I0754778

THE PRAYER EXPERIMENT

THE PRAYER EXPERIMENT

HOW PRAYING LIKE JESUS REALIGNS EVERYTHING—OUR THOUGHTS, OUR HEARTS, AND OUR POSTURE TOWARD GOD AND THE WORLD

MATT SMALLBONE

ZONDERVAN BOOKS

The Prayer Experiment

Published by Zondervan, 3950 Sparks Drive SE, Suite 101, Grand Rapids, MI 49546, USA. Zondervan is a registered trademark of The Zondervan Corporation, L.L.C., a wholly owned subsidiary of HarperCollins Christian Publishing, Inc.

Requests for information should be addressed to customercare@harpercollins.com.

Zondervan titles may be purchased in bulk for educational, business, fundraising, or sales promotional use. For information, please email SpecialMarkets@Zondervan.com.

ISBN 978-0-310-37273-8 (hardcover)
ISBN 978-0-310-37276-9 (audio)
ISBN 978-0-310-37274-5 (ebook)

Published in association with the literary agency of Smallbone Management.

HarperCollins Publishers, Macken House, 39/40 Mayor Street Upper, Dublin 1, D01 C9W8, Ireland (https://www.harpercollins.com)

Cover design: Micah Kandros
Cover illustrations: Shutterstock
Interior design: Lori Lynch

Printed in the United States of America

26 27 28 29 30 LBC 5 4 3 2 1

To the many folks who taught me to pray: D. Martyn Lloyd-Jones, John M. Frame, Tim Keller, Brother Lawrence, Jon Tyson, Saint Augustine, John Mark Comer, E. M. Bounds, C. S. Lewis, Alpha, Pete Greig, 24-7 Prayer, and The Prayer Course. Thank you for your example, diligent research, and incredible teaching. Your fingerprints are all over this book.

For Mary, Isaac, Caleb, Jack, and Eliana:
This book was shaped by a prayer experiment, but it was lived out with you. Thank you for your patience, your laughter, and your grace along the way. I love you beyond words.

THE LORD'S PRAYER

[Jesus said,] "This, then, is how you should pray:

"'Our Father in heaven,
hallowed be your name,
your kingdom come,
your will be done,
  on earth as it is in heaven.
Give us today our daily bread.
And forgive us our debts,
  as we also have forgiven our debtors.
And lead us not into temptation,
  but deliver us from the evil one.'"

—MATTHEW 6:9-13

CONTENTS

INTRODUCTION

THE PRAYER STRUGGLE (YOU ARE HERE)

Have you ever felt like you aren't very good at prayer? You're not alone.

For years, prayer was one of the most frustrating parts of my spiritual life. Honestly, it kind of bored me. Which, I acknowledge, makes me an unlikely candidate to be a pastor, let alone one to write a book about prayer.

And yet here I am, sitting in a Nashville coffee shop, writing about one of the great mysteries of life: how human beings talk with God. Why? Because something has shifted for me in the most beautiful way, and I can't keep it to myself.

Over the last twelve months, prayer has gone from being my greatest struggle to becoming my greatest joy. This is an unexpected twist for someone who if given the choice between a silent retreat and a day at Dollywood would be singing "Jolene" with strangers in line for the Wild Eagle quicker than a Southerner could say "Kenny Rogers." I've always been the guy who chooses fun over tediousness, movement over stillness, and noise over silence. Most of my life has been about chasing good laughs, good times, and good music. This is probably why I spent my late teens through mid-thirties trying to be a rock star.

Yet despite my bent toward loud and fast, somehow talking with God when I am alone has made its way to the top of my priority list. These days prayer brings me both incredible joy and tremendous peace. I now pray many times every day—and I look forward to it!

So what happened? I've discovered that the Lord's Prayer is more than enough to sustain a flourishing prayer life. Why? Because this prayer isn't just a beautiful set of words—it's a blueprint. Jesus makes that clear in the way he introduces it: "This, then, is how you should pray" (Matthew 6:9). In other words, "Pray like this." What's staggering is how complete this prayer is! In just a few short lines, Jesus manages to cover every category of human need and divine concern. There's nothing missing. You can't really add to it; it's all there.

That doesn't mean we're meant only ever to recite the Lord's Prayer word for word and call it a day. Jesus didn't hand out a script so much as he handed us a framework. A pattern to shape our own prayers—and lives—around. It's an outline on which every other prayer can be built.

For the last twelve months, I've leaned on it exclusively to pray through need, joy, grief, fractured relationships, and plenty of late nights worrying about my teenagers. (Teenagers, by the way, are God's way of making sure parents never run out of prayer material. You think you're spiritually mature, then they start driving.)

This prayer has taught me a new way to worship. It's taught me the benefits of daily forgiveness. It has even equipped me for spiritual warfare. Best of all, it has slowly reoriented my heart more completely toward the way of Jesus.

It's a prayer that covers all bases!

For you to understand why I believe this prayer matters so deeply, I need to back up and share a bit of my own journey.

I've been a Christian for over thirty years. I'm a PK (that's church talk for "pastor's kid") from Australia who gave my heart to Jesus as a teenager in a small rural church in the mid-nineties. I moved to the US in 2005 and spent a bunch of years touring as a bass player, playing Jesus music with some of the best people on the planet—folks like Michael W. Smith, Matt Maher, the great Aussie band Alabaster Box, and my talented cousins Rebecca St. James and FOR KING + COUNTRY. For the past decade, I've served as lead pastor of Church of the City, which currently meets in a skate park in downtown Nashville. So, yeah, you could say I have quite the Christian résumé.

But here's the thing. For many of those years, I had a secret: I was a reluctant pray-er. Actually, *reluctant* might not be the right word. I wanted to pray; I just didn't feel like I was very good at it. So I didn't do it much.

Part of the problem? I believed—and still do—in the sovereignty of God. This theological idea teaches that God has the authority, wisdom, and power to do whatever he wants, whenever he wants. That doesn't mean everything that happens is morally God's will, but it does mean nothing surprises him. Which raised a question for me: If God is already going to do what he's going to do, what's the point of prayer? So I pragmatically left the running of the universe up to him—and checked in mostly when disaster hit.

I wasn't against prayer; I just quietly outsourced it to God and called it theology.

But then in 2025 I taught through the Lord's Prayer at my church—and something shifted. During that series, I became so inspired by the genius of this prayer that I decided to try an experiment: This would be the only prayer I'd pray for an entire year. I wanted to see what would happen.

And, friends, it changed me. I became a willing pray-er because I discovered the perfect framework to build my prayers around. I learned that while the Lord's Prayer isn't long, it's deep enough to hold every prayer you'll ever need. I'm learning that you don't need a hundred different prayers—you just need one prayer that can take you to a hundred different places. I haven't encountered a single situation where praying the Lord's Prayer wasn't exactly what was needed. I want that for you too. So consider yourself invited into this grand experiment—an honest, hopeful journey that keeps nudging us from reluctant to willing, from stuck to confident, one prayer at a time.

I'm hardly the first person to wrestle with prayer. Even the great Christians have found it a tremendous struggle. The brilliant David Martyn Lloyd-Jones himself once wrote, "There is nothing that tells the truth about us as Christian people so much as our prayer life. Everything we do in the Christian life is easier than prayer."[1]

Since the very beginning, anytime life becomes precarious, prayer has been humanity's go-to:

YOU DON'T NEED A HUNDRED DIFFERENT PRAYERS— YOU JUST NEED ONE PRAYER THAT CAN TAKE YOU TO A HUNDRED DIFFERENT PLACES.

Students pray before exams, hoping for a passing grade.
Farmers pray for rain, but not too much rain.
Soldiers pray before battle, asking for victory.
Rock stars pray for packed venues and unforgettable shows.
Employees pray before surprise meetings with their bosses.
Athletes pray for the win.
Many of us pray before meals, grateful for what's in front of us.

And yet, for all its familiarity, prayer still feels like a bit of a mystery, doesn't it? I mean, how many of us can honestly say, "You know what? I've got prayer totally figured out. I know exactly when to do it, what to say, and how it works."

For many of us, prayer is a challenge.

Sometimes it feels awkward.
Sometimes it feels like an exercise in futility.
Sometimes it feels like hard work.

And because of that, it can feel easier to skip prayer than to lean in. Why? Well, we all carry our own "prayer barriers." I'll start by sharing a few of mine.

First up, I can become disillusioned by unanswered prayer. Right now, I have several of those just floating around. And at times that has been a massive barrier in my prayer life. I catch myself thinking, "Why even bother? Does anything actually happen when I pray? Why does it feel so haphazard?" Many of us stop praying not because we don't believe in God but because we're not sure it's working.

In addition to that, I'm a guy with a science degree. Which means I even have a barrier related to *answered* prayers, sometimes carrying an antisupernatural bias. My default is often: science first, God second. So even when I do pray and get a preferred outcome, I often assume it was more about medicine, timing, or the placebo effect than anything spiritual.

Another barrier? The story I've told myself about my personality. I've often wondered if the way I'm wired makes me simply not "good" at prayer. As I've already mentioned, I would generally rather distract myself with something fun than sit quietly and bring my pain to God.

I like bingeing Netflix.

I get sidetracked easily.

I have intrusive thoughts at the worst times.

I'll sit down to pray for clarity on a decision, and thirty seconds later I'm researching the Billboard Hot 100 and lamenting the death of real rock bands. Because of this distracted, scattered state, I can easily convince myself that I'm not the kind of person God would use to shape history through prayer.

I know I'm not alone. Some of you believe you'll never be "good" at prayer either. You've seen people who love prayer, and you think, "That's just not me. I'm more of a late-night gaming and Taco Bell guy."

And finally, one of the biggest barriers I (and probably you) carry into prayer is my image of God.

In his excellent work *The Problem of Pain,* C. S. Lewis notes that what we really seem to want is a God who looks at whatever we feel like doing and shrugs: "If it makes them happy, what's the harm?" He wrote, "We want, in fact, not so much a Father in

Heaven as a grandfather in heaven—a senile benevolence who, as they say, 'liked to see young people enjoying themselves,' and whose plan for the universe was simply that it might be truly said at the end of each day, 'a good time was had by all.'"[2]

For some people, God is warm, soft-spoken, and utterly unwilling to discipline anyone about anything. Others imagine God as a sort of heavenly vending machine: Punch in the right prayer with enough faith, and out comes whatever blessing you ordered. And then there's the view of God as a cosmic cop—always watching, ready to blow the whistle the moment you step out of line.

When it comes to how we approach prayer, our view of God is important because, for example, we'll never be vulnerable and honest with God if we don't think he can be trusted. The way we view God massively impacts how we talk to him. If you don't think God is kind, trustworthy, or near, why would you ever open up to him?

So how about you? What gets in the way when you try to pray? Because you're reading this, chances are you have a complicated relationship with prayer too. That's okay. I'm genuinely glad you're holding this book in your hands. My hope is simple: that what we discover together in these pages will breathe fresh energy into your prayer life, just as it has into mine.

In the coming chapters, I want to walk you through the journey of how this ancient prayer can shape every prayer you ever pray. Here's how it will work: Each chapter unpacks a small section of the Lord's Prayer, paired with a simple practice you can try for yourself. My hope is that together, we'll break through barriers and learn to pray with confidence, moving from reluctant pray-ers to willing and joyful ones. By the end, I hope you'll be ready to take up the thirty-day prayer challenge, knowing you are engaging in a practice that is powerful and transformative.

The genius of the Lord's Prayer is that it's simple enough for a toddler to memorize yet profound enough to serve you for a lifetime.

But first—before we get to all that—a quick word about how *not* to pray.

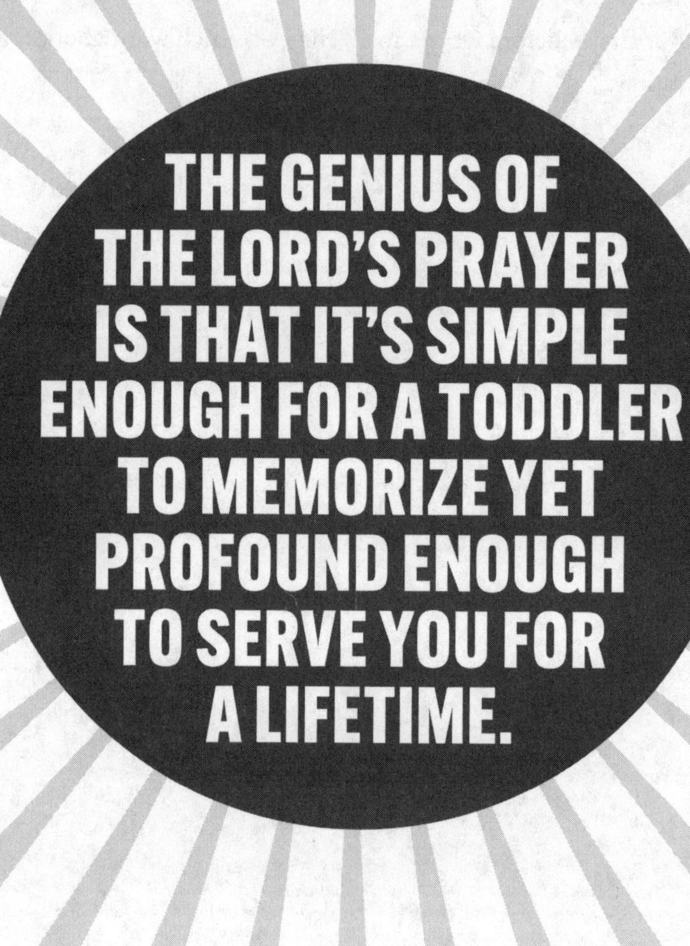
THE GENIUS OF
THE LORD'S PRAYER
IS THAT IT'S SIMPLE
ENOUGH FOR A TODDLER
TO MEMORIZE YET
PROFOUND ENOUGH
TO SERVE YOU FOR
A LIFETIME.

ONE

HOW *NOT* TO PRAY

When I was a kid, I used to pray every night for a new bicycle. Then I realized the Lord doesn't work that way—so I stole one and asked Him to forgive me.

—EMO PHILIPS

In his famous Sermon on the Mount, Jesus teaches his disciples what it means to be fully human. In it, he offers a radical new vision of life in the kingdom of God. This isn't just moral advice; it's a framework for human flourishing. And right in the middle of this sermon—just after talking about giving to the poor and just before talking about fasting—Jesus hits pause and teaches them how to pray.

But before he shows them how to pray, he starts by telling them how not to. It's a bold move. These are Jewish men, raised in a culture where prayer is as normal as breathing. Most have been reciting daily prayers since they could speak. They have structured prayer times, memorized liturgies, and centuries of tradition under their belts. Prayer isn't just something they do—it's part of who they are.

So for Jesus to step in and say, "You're doing it wrong"—well, that's kind of like telling Jimi Hendrix he's holding his guitar the wrong way. You'd better have something really good to say next.

Jesus does.

So what exactly does he say about the wrong way to pray? Let's take a look at Matthew 6:5: "When you pray, *do not be like the hypocrites*, for they love to pray standing in the synagogues and on the street corners to be seen by others. Truly I tell you, they have received their reward in full" (emphasis added).

According to Jesus, the first mistake in prayer is praying like a hypocrite. The word *hypocrite* (*hypokritēs*) originally referred to Greek actors who wore masks to play different roles.[1] In this context, Jesus is criticizing the religious leaders—especially the Pharisees—for a certain kind of hypocrisy: They did outwardly good and religious things, but those actions hid the brokenness within them.

Their problem wasn't about praying the wrong words; it was about praying with the wrong heart. They were doing the *right thing* with the *wrong motive*. They weren't really talking to God; they were talking *at* God—all while knowing an audience was listening in.

In Luke 18:11–12, Jesus tells a parable that captures this hypocrisy perfectly. He quotes a Pharisee praying: "God, I thank you that I am not like other people—robbers, evildoers, adulterers—or even like this tax collector. I fast twice a week and give a tenth of all I get."

Jesus is essentially saying, "Yeah . . . that's not it."

Now, we may not use the same words as that Pharisee, but let's be honest—we've all met (or been) the twenty-first-century version of this guy. He's the dude praying in the small group circle who sounds more like he's preaching a mini sermon than talking to God.

Some people pray in Greek: "Lord, as I was serving you through *diakonia* this week, I just felt your *rhēma* word confirming that in this postmodern cultural moment . . ."

Which is fine . . . I guess. But here's the thing: God already knows Greek—and sociology. You don't need to impress him with it. Again, it's not that quoting Greek or sociology is wrong (I'm a big fan of both!). It's just that prayer isn't meant to be a spiritual TED Talk. If we're more concerned about sounding holy or looking smart than we are about being honest, we've missed the point.

Jesus makes it clear: Our motivation in prayer matters deeply.

If you zoom out and look at the broader context of the Sermon on the Mount, Jesus keeps hitting this same note: *Real righteousness is about the heart, not the performance.* Giving, fasting, and praying have spiritual power only when they flow from a sincere heart.

So Jesus begins his teaching on prayer with this caution: *Don't pray to impress people. Don't pray for applause. Don't pray to be seen.* And then he offers an antidote to performative prayer: "When you pray, go into your room, close the door and pray to your Father, who is unseen" (Matthew 6:6).

Now, the power of prayer isn't found in simply shutting your bedroom door. We know that because when Jesus prays elsewhere in the New Testament, you don't see him locking himself in a

CONNECTION—
REAL CONNECTION—
REQUIRES SPACE.
INTIMACY NEEDS
INTENTIONALITY.

quiet room. For most of his ministry years, he was living the carny life—couch surfing, staying with friends, sharing spaces with his disciples. He didn't exactly have a guest suite with a "prayer closet."

But what you do see, time and time again, is Jesus removing himself from the noise. Heading out into the wilderness. Climbing a hillside. Stepping away from the crowds. "Close the door" is a metaphor to highlight the importance of privacy. This emphasizes the idea that prayer is about the inner life, the heart—it's about having a genuine, intimate connection with God. That's the true core of prayer, whether it happens in public or in private. And clearly Jesus isn't against public prayer, since he himself prayed publicly at times. The point he's making isn't architectural. Rather, he is showing us that when we pray, we need to create a space where we can focus. A space where we can be alone with the Father—no audience, no distractions, no pressure to impress. A space private enough that we can be vulnerable and pray honest prayers.

I've learned this the hard way in my marriage. My wife, Mary, and I have discovered that if the only conversations we have are around our kids, we have to keep things pretty surface level, which easily leads to feeling disconnected from each other. We're at our best—most connected, most alive—when we carve out time to be alone together. Not being surrounded by noise. Not coordinating logistics. Just spending time together in the quiet.

It's the same with God. You can go your entire life talking *at* God and never feel close to him. Why? Because connection—real connection—requires space. Intimacy needs intentionality.

That's what Jesus is getting at when he says to go into your room and shut the door. He's saying to get alone with your heavenly Father. Strip away the show. *Don't pray to impress people. Don't pray like a hypocrite hoping someone nearby thinks, "Wow . . . that guy can really pray."* Instead, pull away. Get quiet. Make space. Just be with the Father. When we do this regularly, something authentic happens: Hypocrisy loses its grip on our prayer lives, and we stop performing for the Christians within earshot.

The second mistake in prayer is "praying like a pagan." (Which, by the way, would be a dark—but highly marketable—album title for a progressive rock band.) Jesus warns against praying in this way in Matthew 6:7: "When you pray, *do not keep on babbling like pagans*, for they think they will be heard because of their many words" (emphasis added).

Pagans thought that the more words you used, the more you could manipulate the gods to act.[2] They tried to prove their sincerity through intensity and by babbling on endlessly. Prayer became performance art designed to coerce. It's as if they believed that if they found the right formula, the divine vending machine would be manipulated into delivering a big ol' bag of candy.

Jesus says that's not how it works.

When we pray like pagans, we act as if God is reluctant. As if we have to badger or convince him to care. But prayer isn't a hostage negotiation. It's not spiritual arm-twisting. And yet, if we're honest, many of us have prayed this way. I know I have. We try to bargain. We overexplain. We pile up words hoping that maybe this time God will do what we want.

But here's the hard truth: *We can't control God by the volume and intensity of our words.* We don't force his hand with longer prayers, louder voices, or more spiritual-sounding language. Ecclesiastes 5:2 puts it plainly: "God is in heaven and you are on earth, so let your words be few." In other words, eloquence is overrated. Word count doesn't impress God. Shouting won't get his attention faster.

And then, just when we think we might be a little clearer on what prayer is all about, Jesus throws one of his famous curveballs in Matthew 6:8: "Do not be like them, for your Father knows what you need before you ask him." At this point, some of us can't help but think, "Wait a minute, God. If you already know what I need, then why should I bother praying at all?"

If that has crossed your mind, congratulations—you're standing right on the edge of a life-changing breakthrough in how you think about prayer. You're beginning to see that prayer was never meant to be transactional—an exchange of requests and results. Yes, Jesus later invites us to ask for daily bread, but he's showing us that the heart of prayer isn't about getting things *from* God—it's about being *with* God.

Maybe the real reward of prayer is this: The God of the universe, who already knows your needs, still wants to meet with you. To draw you into intimacy and connection. To form you in the quiet, behind closed doors, where it's just you and your Father. So Jesus invites us into a radically different kind of prayer. A relational kind. A grounded kind. One that reflects who God actually is.

One of my favorite definitions of prayer comes from Dallas Willard: "Prayer is intelligent conversation about matters of mutual concern."[3] In other words, prayer is what happens when two parties in a relationship talk honestly about what's going on. Jesus is reframing not just how people pray but how they view God. This moment in the Sermon on the Mount isn't just a prayer tutorial, it's a total shift in how humans relate to the divine. It's about me talking to God about things that matter—to both of us!

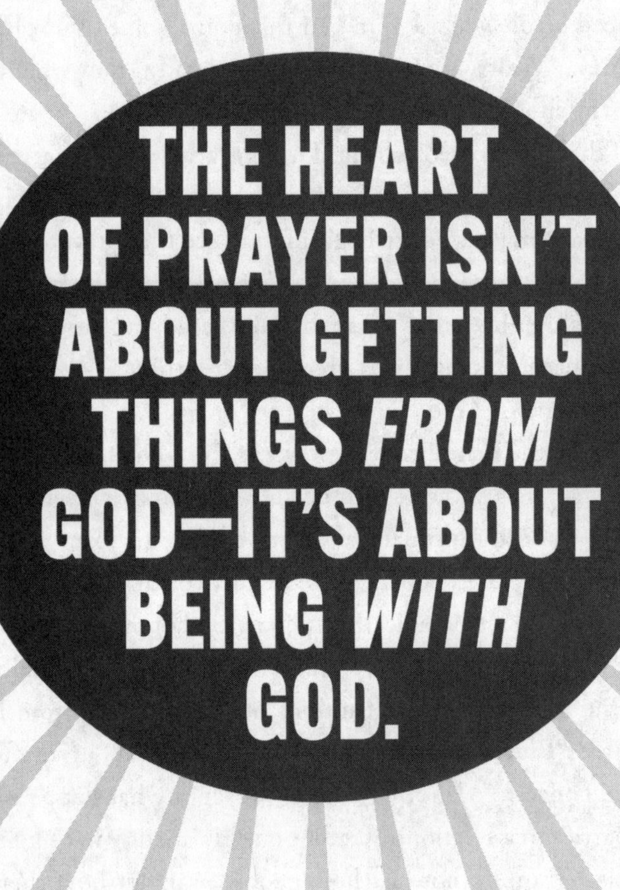
THE HEART
OF PRAYER ISN'T
ABOUT GETTING
THINGS *FROM*
GOD—IT'S ABOUT
BEING *WITH*
GOD.

Which is why some of the best advice on prayer I've ever received came from my friend Jon Tyson: *Pray what you've got.* Nothing more, nothing less.

If you've ever sat down to pray and thought, "I don't even know what to say," you're not alone. The Bible is full of people who went to God with whatever came to mind—fear, frustration, confusion, gratitude—and God met them there. Prayer doesn't have to be polished. Sometimes the most authentic prayers sound more like sighs than sentences. Let me show you what I mean. Hannah once prayed so passionately that the priest thought she was drunk: "In her deep anguish Hannah prayed to the LORD, weeping bitterly. . . . As she kept on praying to the LORD, Eli observed her mouth. Hannah was praying in her heart, and her lips were moving but her voice was not heard. Eli thought she was drunk and said to her, 'How long are you going to stay drunk? Put away your wine'" (1 Samuel 1:10, 12–14).

No script. No fancy language. Just tears and quivering lips. And God heard every bit of it.

King David? He was a first-ballot Hall of Famer of "Pray what you've got." I still chuckle when I read Psalm 22:6: "I am a worm and not a man . . ." That, folks, is praying what you've got.

Moses, the overwhelmed and frustrated leader, once blurted, "Why have you brought this trouble on your servant? . . . I cannot carry all these people by myself; the burden is too heavy for me" (Numbers 11:11, 14). He didn't hide his limits—and God didn't shame him for them. God responded by giving him help.

Then there's the tax collector in Jesus's story—a simple man standing in the back of the temple, too ashamed to look up: "God, have mercy on me, a sinner" (Luke 18:13). Just seven words. No

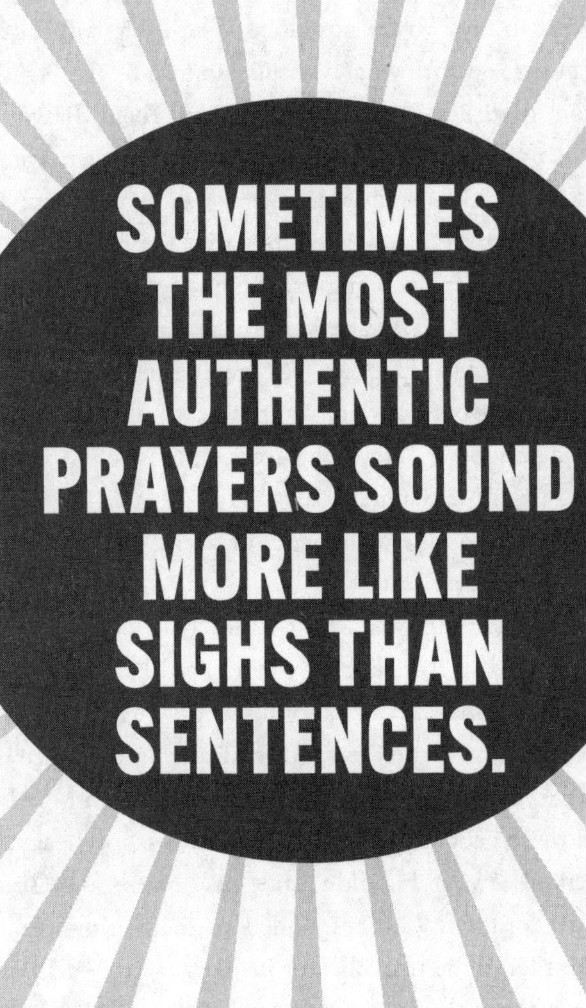
SOMETIMES
THE MOST
AUTHENTIC
PRAYERS SOUND
MORE LIKE
SIGHS THAN
SENTENCES.

performance, no pretending. Jesus said that man went home right with God.

And Jesus himself prayed honestly: "Father, if you are willing, take this cup from me; yet not my will, but yours be done" (Luke 22:42).

If the Son of God could bring his full heart—fear, surrender, and trust—so can we. Here's the point: Prayer isn't about saying the right thing with a lot of words; it's about saying something true. It's about bringing your whole self—your thoughts, your emotions, your silence—into God's presence. If all you can manage is a sigh or a few awkward words, that's enough. The Bible makes it clear: God isn't grading your grammar; he's after your heart. C. S. Lewis said it like this: "We must lay before Him what is in us, not what ought to be in us."[4]

Don't pray what you think God wants to hear. That's what the Pharisees did. Don't babble to impress or manipulate. That's what the pagans did. Just pray honestly and authentically.

Scripture is full of broken people offering prayers that are raw, varied, honest. And that's the point. We need to learn to pray honestly—in all kinds of situations. And yeah, it might be messy. Some prayers will be beautiful. Some will be broken. Some will be both. Bring it all in prayer. I promise you God can handle it. Even if your motives are mixed, even if your faith feels wobbly, even if you have only raw words—pray what you've got.

PRACTICAL PRAYER TIPS

Let's get practical. "Pray what you've got" might sound something like this:

- "God, my phone's search history is a mess. I'm struggling with lust. Help."
- "Jesus, I'm falling apart over here. My marriage is on the ropes. I need you."
- "Lord, my kids are driving me insane, and I don't know what to do. Please help."

These kinds of prayers are messy. And real. That's the type of prayer that Jesus is inviting us into.

Try it today.

Be still for a moment.

Find a quiet place.

And simply *pray what you've got* for a minute or two.

TWO

THE ATTENTIVE FATHER

This, then, is how you should pray:

"*Our Father* . . ."

—MATTHEW 6:9, EMPHASIS ADDED

The only person who dares wake up a king at 3:00 a.m. for a glass of water is a child. We have that kind of access.

—TIM KELLER

In Luke 11:1, we read about this fascinating moment: "One day Jesus was praying in a certain place. When he finished, one of his disciples said to him, 'Lord, teach us to pray, just as John taught his disciples.'"

This scene gets me every time. Jesus is praying—and his disciples are watching. They had grown up praying. They knew the prayers. But something about the way Jesus prayed stopped them in their tracks. There was something different. Something alive. Something incredibly compelling. So they say, "Jesus, whatever *that* is—teach us how to do it." And in response, Jesus gives them what we now call the Lord's Prayer.

Please get this: *The Lord's Prayer is not a script to recite—it's a framework to live by.* Yes, it's worth memorizing. Yes, there is power in repeating it thoughtfully. But Jesus wasn't just giving us words to say. He was offering us a template for a healthy, powerful, vibrant prayer life.

When we pray this prayer with intentionality, it realigns everything—our thoughts, our hearts, our posture toward God and the world. It's that powerful. So for the rest of this book, we're going to take our time walking through it, one phrase at a time. We'll explore what each line means, how it helps us relate to God, and how it can reshape our prayers in everyday life.

But first, let's talk structure. The Lord's Prayer is made up of six movements. The first three are God-focused. The last three are human-focused. This pattern isn't random; rather, most scholars believe this ordering is deeply intentional. It's a subtle yet beautiful reminder that healthy prayer doesn't begin with our needs. It begins with God—his nature, his kingdom, his will. This first part of the prayer is what theologians call adoration.[1]

Let's pick it up in Matthew 6:9, right after Jesus finishes telling his disciples how not to pray: "This, then, is how you should pray: 'Our Father . . .'"

My prayers didn't used to start out like that. Instead, they sounded more like this: "Dear Jesus, here's how I need you to bail me out of this weird situation in the next fifteen seconds or

THE LORD'S
PRAYER IS NOT
A SCRIPT TO
RECITE—IT'S A
FRAMEWORK TO
LIVE BY.

so . . ." But Jesus enters prayer differently. He doesn't begin with a request. He begins with a relationship. He says, when you pray, start by addressing God as Father.

Pause and let that sink in.

Jesus doesn't speak to God like he's some cosmic force or distant deity.

He doesn't start with, "O Sovereign Lord of Angel Armies."

He says simply, "Father." And not just his Father—*our* Father.

That's a massive shift. New Testament scholar Joachim Jeremias points out something fascinating: In all of Jewish literature up to that point, there's no record of anyone addressing God directly as Father. The closest you'd get would be terms like Lord or Master.

But Jesus? He calls God *Abba*, the Aramaic equivalent of "Dad" or "Papa."

Jeremias writes,

> "Abba" was the address of the small child to his father. And the Talmud confirms this when it says: "When a child experiences the taste of wheat [that is, when it is weaned], it learns to say 'Abba' ['dear father'] and 'Imma' ['dear mother']" (b. Ber. 40; b. Sanh. 70b). "Abba" and "Imma" are thus the first sounds that the child stammers. But these terms were not limited to small children; grown sons and daughters also used them to address their parents. "Abba" was an everyday word, a homey family word, a secular word, the tender, filial address to a father: "Dear father." No Jew would have dared to address God in this manner. Jesus did it always.[2]

In other words, Jesus talked to God like a kid talks to a loving parent: with affection, with trust, with closeness.

And then Jesus turns around and says you can talk to God that way too.

That's the first thing Jesus wants us to know about prayer:

It's not a performance.
It's not a ritual.
It's a relationship.

We don't begin by groveling to some distant deity power broker in an alternate universe. We begin by coming home. This is good news.

Even so, after years of pastoring, I know that the idea of calling God "Father" can stir up some heavy feelings. As it turns out, the word *Father* can bring either warmth or a mild existential crisis, depending on your upbringing. It's one of the few words that can function as both a prayer starter and the impetus to call to one's therapist, because not everyone had a great dad. This is why you might wince when someone starts their prayer with "Papa" or—brace yourself—"Daddy God." You hate it. Not because you're cynical but because your dad wasn't there for you when you needed him. Or maybe he hurt you. And now you're doing the courageous, exhausting work of healing. You're sitting in counseling rooms, facing that pain head-on, trying to untangle the mess. I just want to say I'm so sorry for your pain.

For others of you, maybe it's not about the father you had; it's about the father you are. Maybe you feel like you're failing.

Maybe you carry shame. And so this metaphor of God as Father just feels . . . complicated. If that's you, I see you.

This part of the Lord's Prayer may take the most heart work. But I believe it's worth it. Because Jesus isn't asking us to imagine our earthly fathers and then assume God is a bigger-than-life version of them. He's pointing us to something entirely better. He's inviting us to imagine a perfect Father: attentive, present, compassionate, kind, patient, wise, loving—and highly accessible.[3]

For those whose experiences with fathers were hurtful—or nonexistent—this is where healing begins. This may be the moment when, as psychologists say, the reparenting begins. My prayer is that as you open yourself up to God as Father, you'll receive what you missed out on. That he will heal and fulfill the emotional and spiritual needs that went unmet in your earliest years. Because this matters. A lot. The image you carry of God shapes the way you pray. And the way you live.

If you picture God as a distant, disappointed authority figure—always mad, always frowning—it's no wonder you're hesitant to pray. Who wants to approach someone like that? Or maybe your image of God is the opposite: a cosmic "yes man," a heavenly pushover who nods along with every harebrained scheme you've ever concocted. That might feel nice for a while, but deep down, you'll struggle to trust a God who never challenges you. Because here's the truth: Good fathers sometimes say no. And when they do, it's not necessarily because they're angry—it's because they love you. Boundaries help kids thrive. They create safety and peace. So if you're a teenager reading this and your parents said no to you this week, take it as a sign of love. Because honestly, it's

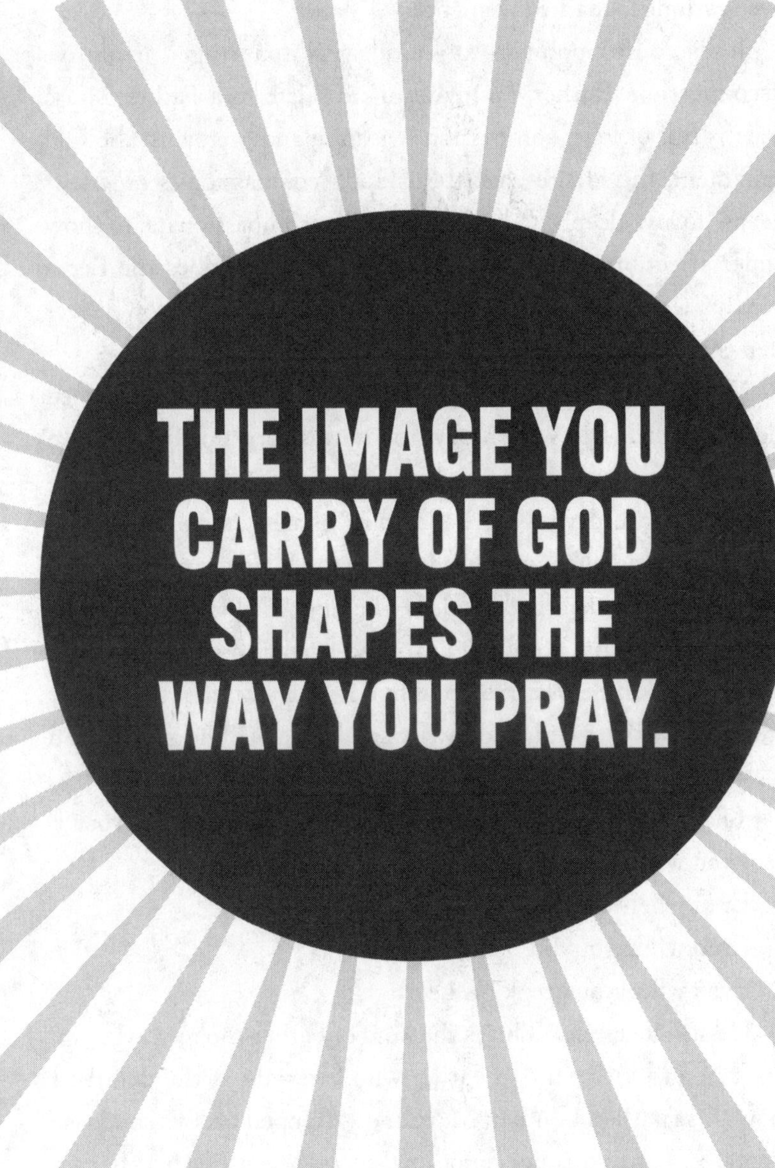
THE IMAGE YOU
CARRY OF GOD
SHAPES THE
WAY YOU PRAY.

way easier to say yes to everything your kids ask of you. But real love is stronger than convenience.

Jesus doesn't point us to a God with toxic anger or passive disconnection. Rather, he invites us to relate to a Father whose heart is full of love, compassion, wisdom, and mercy. In the Old Testament, the Hebrew word for God's compassion is *raham*. It means "to love deeply, to have mercy, to be compassionate, to show tender affection."[4] It's a word that perfectly describes the fierce love that a parent feels for their newborn child. And if you've ever been there, you know what I mean.

When our firstborn son, Isaac, was born, we were overwhelmed and exhausted. My wife Mary's body was torn up. Postpartum hormones were kicking in. We hadn't slept for more than a ninety-minute block in days. Isaac had tummy issues and wouldn't stop crying. And yet when we looked down at that tiny, wrinkled, loud little human, our hearts exploded. The moment I saw him, I realized that up to that point my heart had been two sizes too small. I loved that kid deeply. He brought out layers of affection in my father's heart that I didn't know I was capable of. The first second I saw him, I knew I was willing to give my life for him.

That's *raham*. That's what God feels when he looks at you.

Even when you're a mess.

Even when you are loud and unreasonable.

Even when you did *that* thing.

Even when you break his heart.

He still loves you. This is the kind of Father you're praying to.

He's also an attentive Father who cares about the details. I know this firsthand. When Mary and I dropped off our son Isaac at college, it was a super-emotional day—because it had been a super-long journey to get him there. Here's why: As Isaac grew older, we noticed that he was quite different from his siblings. He had limited interests. He *loved* watching *Wild Kratts*, baseball, and the band U2. To this day, he really only listens to three bands: U2, FOR KING + COUNTRY, and Walk the Moon (but only their classic "Shut Up and Dance," which I think we can all agree is an absolute banger). And then we noticed that he has an amazing memory. Like, he can watch a movie a few times and have large scenes memorized. We discovered this the day he—as a three-year-old—started quoting Ham and Phillips from *The Sandlot* when our conservative small group was outside playing baseball.

He inserted himself at catcher and said,

> You mix your Wheaties with your mama's toe jam!
> Yeah!
> You bob for apples in the toilet! And you like it!
> You play ball like a giiirrrrrrrl!
> What did you say?
> You heard me.
> Tomorrow. Noon, at our field. Be there, buffalo-butt breath.

And then came the line that reverberated across the buckle of the Bible Belt:

> Count on it, pee-drinking crap-face!

I looked over at Mary, and I could tell she was horrified. We already felt strange in that group. We were fresh off the plane, new immigrants to the USA. We were surrounded by Americans who seemed to have their lives together and were *very* Christian. The last thing we needed was our kid teaching their kids how to swear. I looked at Isaac and said, "Son! Stop that right now! Where did you learn those horrible words?" That's the moment one of the guys looked at me with tears of laughter streaming down his face and said, "That's a scene from *The Sandlot*. He nailed it!"

I was like, "What's *The Sandlot*?"

Mary said, "It's a movie *your* cousin Luke gave him at Christmas."

I said, "Did you know he could do that? Memorize dialogue?"

Mary looked at me wide-eyed and shook her head. We were equal parts impressed and embarrassed.

As Isaac got older, his memory for facts continued to amaze us. We learned that if he had watched a U2 concert on YouTube a couple of times, he could tell us the set list in the correct order, the guitars that Edge used in each song, and the moment that Bono took off his glasses. Spoiler: It's usually in song three or four. It was the same thing with animal facts. Isaac could talk all day about the differences between an alligator and a crocodile.

But alongside this superpower came some interpersonal struggles. He didn't seem to need friends, at least not in the way that the rest of us in our family did. And he would often say inappropriate things about the way people looked. To this day, if I put on fifteen pounds over the winter and I wear a shirt that's too tight, he'll be the one to tell me about it.

Eventually we realized that the way his mind works probably had a scientific name. It does: autism spectrum disorder. Early on we were told that his moving out of our home as an adult might be an unreasonable expectation. Which brings us back to the day he moved off to college! (I'm not crying . . . you are . . .) The minivan was crammed full—minifridge, boxes, suitcases, DVDs, and an unspoken weight that sat right on my chest. Isaac thrives on routine, and for one month shy of two decades, our family life had revolved around his rhythms. Now we were delivering him to a place where nothing would be familiar: new people, new schedules, new food options that may or may not include pizza every Friday night (his culinary safe zone and emotional anchor).

When we arrived, the campus was swarming with energetic student volunteers grabbing bags and greeting us like we were royalty. I kept glancing at Isaac, waiting for the subtle flicker in his eyes that means "this is too much." But instead, he surprised me. He took a deep breath, squared his shoulders, and marched right toward the mass of loving humanity.

I'd been worried all summer: Would he make friends? Would his professors understand him? Would he know what to do if he became overwhelmed? That's the thing about being a dad—you never stop scanning for danger, even when you know you can't control it.

Shortly after we arrived at check-in, Isaac was greeted by three student mentors who had come back to school early to help him adjust to college life. These warm young Christian men made themselves available to him—however he needed them. Two of them even stayed in his otherwise empty apartment on that first night to help him feel secure!

And then came the goodbye.

Isaac's cohort includes twelve other kids with special needs. Most of us never imagined a future for our kids that involved them not living under our roof, let alone a full-blown on-campus college experience!

So there we were—a bunch of nervous parents living out the very thing we'd prayed for: our kids gaining independence. But knowing it was right didn't make saying goodbye and driving away any easier. Thankfully, the school anticipated this moment and hosted a dance party after dinner. Their goal was simple: to make sure the last thing we saw was our kids having the time of their lives, surrounded by people who genuinely cared for them.

Now, while Isaac has his fair share of challenges, commanding a dance floor is not one of them. So when "Shut Up and Dance" started playing, Mary and I knew this was our moment to say goodbye. It was one of the rare moments when theology and choreography felt equally Spirit-led. As we approached him, Isaac put one hand on the floor and both legs into the air, and the room went nuts. The tears of joy started and a lump formed in my throat. We gave him a quick hug and said, "We'll see you soon, mate!" He rejoined the dance floor by doing some karate moves.

And then we drove home feeling confident that our heavenly Father had lovingly orchestrated this whole thing—right down to the playlist. In that instant, it was as if God whispered to me about Isaac, "I've got him. I'm paying attention. Even more than you are."

Driving away was brutal. But that day became a living reminder: My watchfulness as a father is only a dim reflection of God's watchfulness over his kids. He sees. He notices. He never looks away. So when you close your eyes and whisper, "Our Father," you're reaching out to a God whose love is fierce, compassionate, detail-oriented, and unshakable.

Do you believe this is who God really is? If not, before you go any further in the Lord's Prayer, you'll need to put in some work and wrestle this one to the ground.

You have to fight through the old wounds and false images.

You have to confront the angry, disappointed god in your head.

You have to let go of the passive, disconnected god you've outgrown.

Because the God you imagine is the God you'll pray to. And the God you pray to will shape everything else. If we never unlearn the false images of God that grip our hearts, we'll never be drawn to prayer. But if we do this work—if we take Jesus at his word and say "Our Father" with trust and hope—our hearts will soften. And over time, that will change everything.

"Our Father" isn't just a sweet idea for a Christian tapestry to hang above the piano. This is a healing, transforming, life-changing reality. So when you pray, remember: You're not performing. You're not bargaining. You're reaching out to a Father who sees you, loves you, and delights in you. He has *raham* for you. And if you truly grasp that? You'll never pray the same way again.

One of the deepest barriers to receiving God's love is what many pastors and counselors describe as the *orphan spirit*, a quiet ache in the soul that whispers, "You're on your own."[5] When someone has an orphan spirit, it means they live as though they have no home, no father, no one to catch them if they fall.

And, man, most of us battle this mindset. You can have the right theology—even lead a church—and still carry the ache of spiritual orphanhood: a quiet fear that love might run out, that provision might dry up, that you'll have to earn your place at the table again tomorrow. It's the inner voice always reminding you

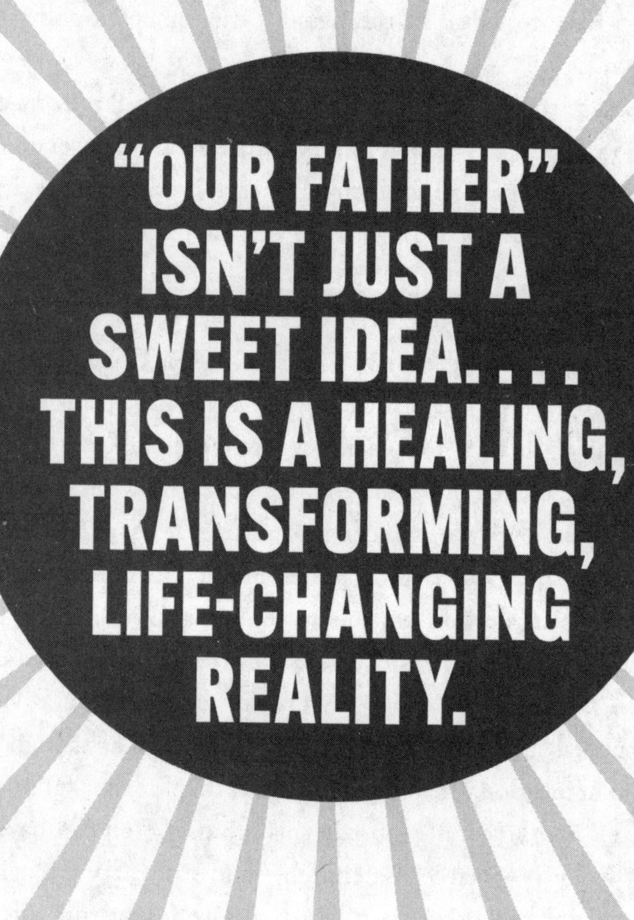
"OUR FATHER"
ISN'T JUST A
SWEET IDEA. . . .
THIS IS A HEALING,
TRANSFORMING,
LIFE-CHANGING
REALITY.

that you are about to be abandoned and alone. Jesus's prayer shatters that lie. When we begin our prayers with "Our Father," we start to believe something truer: that we're no longer orphans. We're adopted sons and daughters of God.

It reminds me of a powerful story I heard once about how love and care can destroy the orphan spirit.[6] After World War II, aid workers were caring for thousands of starving children, many of them orphans who had seen unthinkable things. Even after being rescued and fed, they couldn't sleep. They were afraid that if they drifted off, they'd wake up to another day with no food. So one of the caregivers came up with a simple idea. Each child was given a piece of bread to hold at bedtime—not to eat, just to hold. And that night, for the first time in months, they slept soundly. Because the bread in their hands whispered something their hearts needed to know: "There was food today, and there will be food tomorrow."

Friends, that's what the love of our heavenly Father does. When we finally trust that God will care for us tomorrow—that we're safe, seen, and provided for—we rest.

PRACTICAL PRAYER TIPS

So how do we pray this line: "Our Father"?

Well, let's start here: Don't overthink it. You're not performing. You're not auditioning. You're not sending your words out into a void. You're speaking to someone who already loves you.

Try this: Take a deep breath, get quiet, and simply say out loud, "Father . . ."

Pause there. Let the weight of that word sink in. What does it stir in you? Comfort? Confusion? Resistance? Longing? Gratitude?

Whatever it is, start there. If the idea of God as Father brings pain or baggage, name it. God can handle your honesty. In fact, he invites it. If the word brings comfort, dwell in it. Picture a God who runs to meet you like the father in Luke 15—the one who sees you a long way off and sprints in your direction. This is how you pray "Our Father." Not just with words but with trust, with vulnerability, with hope.

You don't need to impress God—you just need to be with him.

Start your prayer today like this:

Father, I want to know you like Jesus did.
Help me to trust you.
Heal the parts of me that don't believe you're good.
Teach me what it means to be loved by you.

Then sit in silence for a minute or two. Let the truth of how much the Father loves you reshape your heart.

THREE

THE FATHER WHO IS AS CLOSE AS AIR

"Our Father *in heaven* . . ."

—MATTHEW 6:9, EMPHASIS ADDED

The damage done to our practical faith in Christ and in his government-at-hand by confusing heaven with a place in distant or outer space, or even beyond space, is incalculable.

—DALLAS WILLARD

Let's imagine for a moment that you're floating around in the International Space Station, staring back at earth. You're weightless, watching our fragile, blue-green planet suspended in the void. Something happens up there. A shift. Looking down at earth from space, astronauts describe a profound moment when everything changes. The thin veil of atmosphere. The smallness of it all. The stunning connectedness of everything. Suddenly, your problems feel tiny. That passive-aggressive coworker? The tension at home? Even the legitimate rage you feel when a football player says "*The*" before "Ohio State"? It all gets put into perspective. Astronauts call this moment the overview effect.[1] It's a perspective-altering experience that reorders what matters. It recalibrates what is worth worrying about.

The same thing happens in prayer, except the shift has less to do with viewing continents and more to do with realizing your group-text argument wasn't worth the emotional investment. When Jesus taught his disciples to pray, he *began* by helping them pull their eyes off themselves and instead focus their gaze toward God. This shift in how to begin prayer has been very helpful for me. It changes my focus from the microscopic to the majestic. From the chaos of my day to the glory of the Creator. When we start prayer in this manner, it's like trading a microscope for a telescope. We stop obsessing over our own small world and we remember this: There's something bigger. Someone better. Someone more beautiful than we can even comprehend. We remember that God is holy, set apart, worthy of all worship.

When we begin our prayers there, something changes in us. Our posture softens. Our perspective broadens. Our anxiety is interrupted by awe. Just as the overview effect can lead astronauts to return home with a fresh sense of purpose, adoration reshapes how we see our lives, our problems, and even ourselves. So let's move forward two words into the Lord's Prayer: "in heaven." When many of us think of heaven, we imagine a fluffy cloud city in the sky, and maybe Saint Peter at the pearly gates, clipboard in hand, checking résumés and sin reports. But the Greek word Jesus uses here, *ouranos*, literally means "the heavens." In the first century, *ouranos* referred to the sky—the atmosphere, the vaulted expanse above us.[2] But the word has a broad semantic range. In fact, the translators of the King James Version often rendered *ouranos* with the most ordinary of terms: "air."[3] Dallas Willard picked up on this nuance, and he believed it carried profound implications for how we understand God's nearness. He once wrote, "Nothing—no human being or institution, no time, no space, no spiritual being, no event—stands between God and those who trust him. The 'heavens' are always there with you no matter what, and the 'first heaven,' in biblical terms, is precisely the atmosphere or air that surrounds your body."[4] In other words, when Jesus teaches us to pray to "our Father in heaven," he isn't pointing to a distant galaxy. He's pointing to the God who is as close as the air on your skin.

This is why one of my favorite preachers argues that you could just as accurately translate "Our Father in heaven" as "Our Father in the air."[5] And that's wild. Because air is everywhere. It's not just above us—it surrounds us, moves through us, sustains us. There's oxygen in your bloodstream right now. We literally can't live without it. It's a powerful picture: The Father is as close as the air that sustains us!

So when we pray, Jesus is asking us to let go of the distance we sometimes imagine between us and God. He's not inviting us to speak to some far-off deity. He's talking about a God who surrounds us. Who dwells in us. Who is right here. Saint Augustine, whose writings on prayer deeply shaped this book, put it this way:

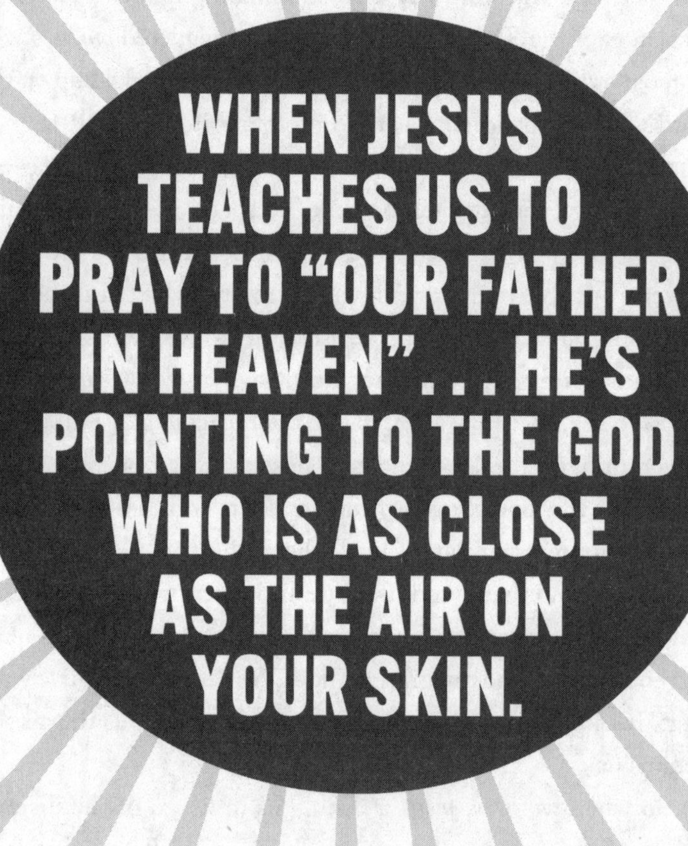
WHEN JESUS
TEACHES US TO
PRAY TO "OUR FATHER
IN HEAVEN" . . . HE'S
POINTING TO THE GOD
WHO IS AS CLOSE
AS THE AIR ON
YOUR SKIN.

"But you were more intimately present to me than I was to myself, and higher than my highest, and more inward than my inward parts."[6]

So here's the big lesson from just these two words—"in heaven": When we pray, we begin by remembering that our Father is intimately close, deeply present, and always near. That reframing is a game changer.

The importance of closeness between humans and God is an idea that Jesus doubles down on in John 15:1–5. To paint a picture for us, he uses an agricultural metaphor, a word picture about a grapevine:

> I am the true vine, and my Father is the gardener. He cuts off every branch in me that bears no fruit, while every branch that does bear fruit he prunes so that it will be even more fruitful. You are already clean because of the word I have spoken to you. Remain in me, as I also remain in you. No branch can bear fruit by itself; it must remain in the vine. Neither can you bear fruit unless you remain in me.
>
> I am the vine; you are the branches. If you remain in me and I in you, you will bear much fruit; apart from me you can do nothing.

Here's how it works. The vine represents Jesus. We're the branches. The branches are connected to the vine, and the "gardener" is God the Father, who lovingly tends and prunes us so that we bear fruit. What fruit? Mere decades later Paul would name this fruit: love, joy, peace, patience, kindness (Galatians 5:22–23)—all that good stuff.

But the key word in this passage is "remain" (your translation may use the word "abide"). Jesus says it four times in just the first few verses. He will eventually use it eleven times before he has finished teaching the true vine metaphor! It's almost as if we need to pay attention because "remaining in the vine" seems to matter a lot to Jesus. The Greek word for "remain" is *menō*, meaning "to stay, to remain, to continue to be present, to be held continually."[7] It's a beautiful image of ongoing presence—of staying close, staying connected, staying held. So when Jesus says, "Remain in me," he's saying, "Stay with me. Abide in me. Let me hold you."

And that's the same picture he paints in the Lord's Prayer. God isn't distant. He's not "up there." He's right here, like the air in your lungs, like the sap in a vine. His life flows through you when you stay connected to him.

When my daughter, Ellie, was little, she loved being held. Some nights she'd crawl into my lap and just want to sit there, not talking, not moving, just being. And in those moments, something in both of us would settle. That's what remaining feels like—being so close that words sometimes become unnecessary. That's the fruit Jesus wants for us. The fruit of connection. The fruit of intimacy. Because honestly, some of the crankiest Christians you'll ever meet are people who've done plenty of singing and sermon-listening and maybe even some volunteering—but very little being held by Jesus. To remain is to rest in his nearness. It's to remember that *our Father in heaven* is not far beyond the clouds but as close as the air that swirls around us.

Corrie ten Boom once wrote about a moment in the Ravensbrück concentration camp that changed the way she understood God's presence.[8] She and her sister Betsie were surrounded

TO REMAIN IS
TO REST IN HIS
NEARNESS.

by fear and death in a place that felt as far from heaven as you can imagine. One night, in the middle of that darkness, Betsie quietly prayed the Lord's Prayer. Her voice trembled: "Our Father, who art in heaven . . ." As Corrie listened, something shifted. The air in that filthy barrack seemed to thicken with peace. It was as if heaven itself had entered the room—invisible, but undeniably there. Later, Corrie would write, "There is no pit so deep that God's love is not deeper still."[9]

That's the power of the words "Our Father in heaven." He's not a Father far away in the clouds but a Father whose presence fills even the darkest places. And here's some *great* news: That same presence Corrie and Betsie felt in the barracks isn't reserved for extraordinary moments of suffering. It's available to us right here, right now. Prayer is how we tune our hearts to that reality. It's how we remember that God's nearness isn't something we earn or chase; it's something we notice.

Sometimes that noticing happens in the quiet of the morning. Sometimes in a deep breath before a meeting. Sometimes in the middle of chaos, when you whisper, "Our Father in heaven," and realize he's closer than the air itself.

PRACTICAL PRAYER TIPS

Prayer begins by remembering that God is closer than we think—nearer than breath itself.

When we slow down enough to notice that nearness, something in us settles. Here are a few simple ways to practice that today.

1. Slow your breathing.

   Before you speak, take a few deep breaths.

   Breathe in God's presence.

   Breathe out your worries.

2. Instead of starting with what you need, start with who God is.

   Tell him what you love about him. Let awe have the first word.

3. Picture the vine.

   Imagine yourself as a branch connected to the vine—rooted, steady, alive.

   You don't have to force fruit to grow. You just stay connected, and life flows through you.

4. Keep it simple.

   You don't have to sound holy or poetic. Prayer isn't about performance—it's about presence.

   Try a one-sentence prayer:

   "God, I'm here."

   "Jesus, hold me."

   "Spirit, fill me."

5. Let silence do the heavy lifting.

   When you run out of words, stay there.

   Remaining is often wordless.

   Sit with God. Let the quiet remind you that you're safe, seen, and held.

   If your mind starts to wander, simply return to your breath—the air that sustains you—and whisper, "Our Father in heaven . . . closer than the air I breathe."

FOUR

THE RESPECTED AND ASTONISHING FATHER

"Our Father in heaven,
hallowed be your name . . ."
—MATTHEW 6:9, EMPHASIS ADDED

If you understand it, it isn't God.
—SAINT AUGUSTINE

When I was little, I thought "hallowed be your name" meant God's name was Harold. For years I thought we Methodists were all super committed to this Harold guy. But as I've aged, I've come to learn that *hallow* is a verb meaning "to respect greatly."[1] So to hallow God's name is to say, "There is no one like you. You are one of a kind. There's nothing more worthy, more beautiful, more sacred than you."

So what does that look like when we pray? Pastor Timothy Keller, one of my favorite voices on all things Jesus, says that to hallow God's name is to have a heart of grateful joy toward God and to experience a wondrous sense of his beauty.[2] Let's just sit with that for a second. Because that's in stark contrast to how most of us pray. For many, prayer becomes a spiritual vending machine where we insert our needs and hope for custom solutions. But hallowing God's name is different. It's about turning our attention away from what we want and toward who he is.

To be fair, most of us weren't taught to pray that way. I mean, how often do we sit in stillness and adore God? No shame here—this isn't about guilt. I've been there too. But I've come to understand that many of us haven't yet discovered the depth of prayer that Jesus invites us into: When we learn to hallow God's name, our hearts change. According to Jesus, prayer begins with adoration—worshipping a God so beautiful, good, and loving that even a glimpse of him makes everything else fade into the background. Adoration is a massive perspective shift; it's like seeing earth from space. And once you've had that view, you can't unsee it.

But life often pulls us in the other direction. We zoom in on the details: problems, emotions, to-do lists. We forget to look up. That was especially true for me as a guy who's wired more toward logic and science.

But awe and reason aren't enemies. Sometimes they even walk hand in hand. Take Dr. Francis Collins, the physician-geneticist who led the Human Genome Project. Early in his career, Collins was an atheist. To him, the human body was just a series of mechanisms: cells, molecules, systems. But then something shifted.

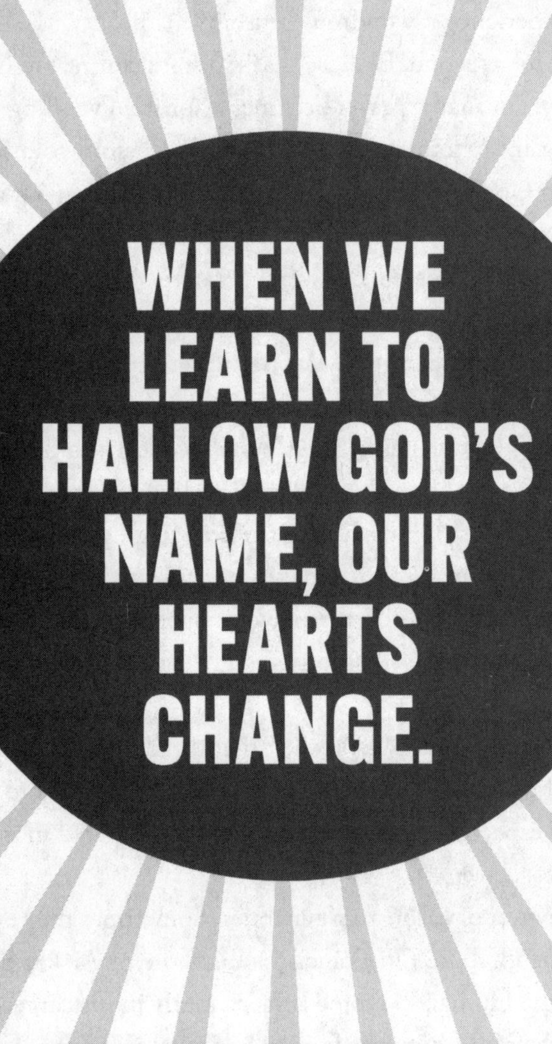
WHEN WE
LEARN TO
HALLOW GOD'S
NAME, OUR
HEARTS
CHANGE.

One night, after a breakthrough in genome research, he stepped outside and looked up at the stars. The vastness. The staggering complexity. It overwhelmed him. He experienced his own version of the overview effect.

In that moment, surrounded by wonder, he realized that none of this could be accidental. The genetic code, the harmony of cells, the very structure of life—it all pointed to a Creator. He dropped to his knees in adoration. He went on to say that the night sky's elegance and complexity point to "an intelligence far beyond anything we can create."[3] His scientific journey didn't lead him away from God—it led him into deep, awe-filled worship.

And here's the truth for all of us: Everyday miracles are all around us. But they've become so familiar, we stop noticing. When's the last time you stood under the stars—and looked up? It's a real perspective changer. This is one of the great gifts of the Australian outback at night. There are no city lights, no noise, just an unfiltered sky. The Milky Way is so bright it looks painted on, and the Southern Cross hangs steady in the darkness as a quiet reminder that God's world is immense and beautiful.

That's adoration—being in the presence of a great God and remembering how small we are and yet how loved we are. So when Jesus teaches us to pray, "Our Father in heaven, hallowed be your name," we need to notice that the prayer doesn't start with us and our needs. It starts with adoring God. It's saying, "God, before I ask for anything, I just want to remember how amazing you are." And when my prayer starts here, it reorients my heart. It becomes less about what I need and more about who God is. Over the last twelve months, praying this line has changed the transactional nature of my previous relationship with God. I now look forward to getting alone with God and sitting in his presence.

It reminds me of when I first started dating my wife. I didn't pursue her because I wanted something from her; I pursued her because she captivated me. She was different. She was special. I'd never met anyone like her. When I was seventeen, I fell in love with Mary (we called her "Mezza" back then . . . because Australia) at our coed boarding school in Toowoomba, Australia. We were in the eleventh grade when I first realized there was something different about her. This was back in the days before cell phones, so our early romance unfolded through a steady stream of handwritten notes passed between classes. I still have a bunch of them tucked away in my bedside drawer.

For weeks I tried to decode them like sacred texts. Does she like me? Or like-like me? One day she signed off with "Love, Mary," and I was convinced it was destiny. The next day she went back to just "Mary," and I spiraled into an existential crisis.

Then one Friday a group of us went to see a movie together—a sweet little romantic flick called *Jurassic Park*. I had a plan. My friend also liked Mary, so there was competition for the seat beside her. I maneuvered like a Navy SEAL, and by the time she chose her row, I had secured the spot directly to her right. About halfway through the movie, I noticed her right hand resting on the armrest, just behind the cupholder. It was now or never. So while a large dinosaur ate a smaller dinosaur, I made my move. We held hands *through* that cupholder for the rest of the movie. It was electric. I thought, "This is it. Happily ever after."

False.

When we got back to school, it was awkward. Turns out she

wasn't ready for a relationship, and the only reason she'd held my hand that long was because you can't easily unhold someone's hand through a cupholder without hurting their feelings.

So while I fell in love with Mary in 1993, she didn't feel the same until 1999. We married in 2001. But just like all the good premarriage books tell you, that emotional high doesn't last forever. It's physiologically impossible. Scientists say that the feeling of young love is highly chemical. When you fall in love, your body gets pumped full of dopamine, oxytocin, and serotonin—the same neurochemicals stimulated by taking crack and ecstasy at the same time. Mary and I felt that—for about the first six months of married life. We were kind of high on each other. But slowly the chemicals subsided. And that's when the real work of love began.

Timothy Keller speaks of maturing love this way:

> When over the years someone has seen you at your worst, and knows you with all your strengths and flaws, yet commits him- or herself to you wholly, it is a consummate experience. To be loved but not known is comforting but superficial. To be known and not loved is our greatest fear. But to be fully known and truly loved is, well, a lot like being loved by God. It is what we need more than anything. It liberates us from pretense, humbles us out of our self-righteousness, and fortifies us for any difficulty life can throw at us.[4]

I agree. And more importantly, Scripture agrees! When humans are *both* truly known and loved—whether by a parent, a friend, or ultimately by Jesus—something deep within us settles. And that's what adoration in prayer is like over the course of a

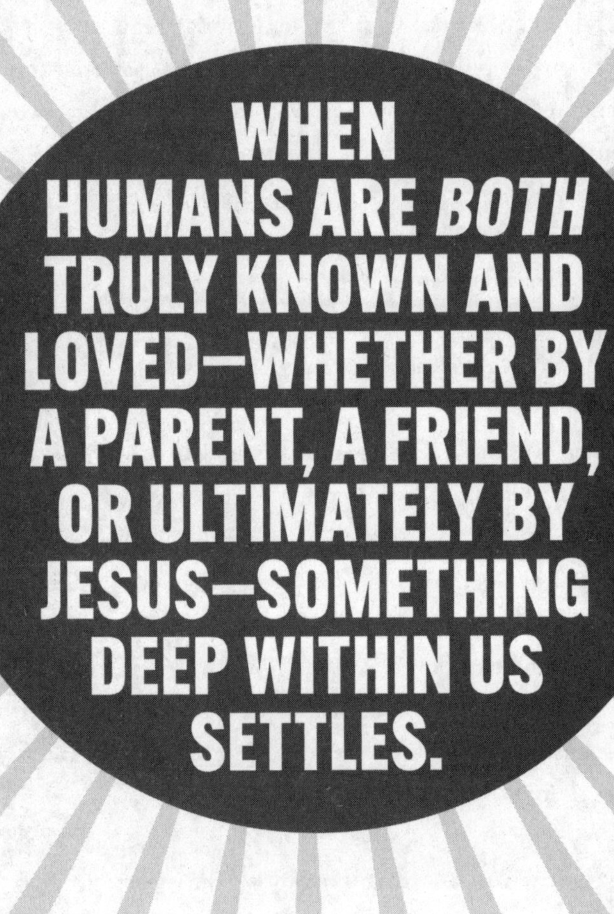
WHEN
HUMANS ARE *BOTH*
TRULY KNOWN AND
LOVED—WHETHER BY
A PARENT, A FRIEND,
OR ULTIMATELY BY
JESUS—SOMETHING
DEEP WITHIN US
SETTLES.

lifetime. It starts with infatuation—with awe and emotion—but matures into something deeper. We gain the inner strength to live with peace, purpose, and generosity. Over time, our relationship with God shifts from excitement about what he gives us to devotion for who he is.

Mature love for God moves from transaction to trust. From thrill to tenderness. From "God, give me" to "God, I love you." And that's exactly where Jesus starts the Lord's Prayer—with adoration. We don't adore God because we want something from him. We adore him because we're captivated by who he is. That might be the biggest shift in my prayer life over the last twelve months. This part of the Lord's Prayer has taught me that prayer is not transactional. Prayer is fundamentally relational. And God is inviting us into a relationship built on adoration.

PRACTICAL PRAYER TIPS

Here's your invitation: Set a timer and spend at least two minutes praying a prayer of adoration.

For some of you, that might not sound like much. For others, it may feel like a stretch. Either way, it's okay. As New Testament scholar John Chapman wisely said, "Pray as you can, not as you can't. Take yourself as you find yourself, and start from that."[5]

Sometimes Jesus prayed all night (Luke 6:12; see also Mark 3:13–15 and John 17:6–9). But don't worry about it if you can't even come close. Pray for one minute if that's where you are.

Start by getting still.

Breathe slowly.

Acknowledge that you're in God's presence.

Then pray the Lord's Prayer out loud, slowly and intentionally:

> Our Father in heaven,
> *hallowed be your name*,
> your kingdom come,
> your will be done,
>   on earth as it is in heaven.
> Give us today our daily bread.
> And forgive us our debts,
>   as we also have forgiven our debtors.
> And lead us not into temptation,
>   but deliver us from the evil one.

Now go back and linger over this phrase: "hallowed be your name."

What comes to mind when you think about the name of God? What words? What images? What memories or feelings?

Here's a helpful practice: Try listing names or titles for God that help you adore him: Creator, Sustainer, Redeemer, Shepherd, Father, Friend.

Speak them out loud, one by one.

Let them become your praise.

Don't rush. Take your time.

You might even pray something like this:

> God, there is no one like you. You are higher than my highest thoughts, deeper than my deepest questions,

stronger than my worst day, and kinder than I could ever deserve.

Hallowed be your name.

And then just be still. Let adoration rise. This is how prayer begins. Not with a grocery list but with a posture of love and a heart turned toward wonder!

FIVE

A CLASH OF KINGDOMS

"Our Father in heaven,
hallowed be your name,
your kingdom come . . ."

—MATTHEW 6:9–10, EMPHASIS ADDED

The Kingdom of God is where we belong.
It is home, and whether we realize it or not,
I think we are all of us homesick for it.

—FREDERICK BUECHNER

Over the last couple of chapters, we've been digging into the specific language Jesus uses to open his prayer. If we were to radically oversimplify it in modern English, it might go something like this: "Our good and kind Papa, who is as close as the air we breathe, holy and precious is your name."

Now Jesus adds the next line: "your kingdom come . . ."

For the longest time, my own prayers sounded more like this:

Oh distant God Almighty,

If you're listening, would you please bend the universe to how I like things done already?

Anyone else?

But here, Jesus turns that instinct upside down.

Instead of us bringing God our list of demands, Jesus teaches us to reorient our hearts with a simple but subversive phrase: "your kingdom come."

So what on earth does it mean? It's a strange phrase. But it's important. If you've read the Gospels, you know Jesus talked constantly about the "kingdom of heaven" or the "kingdom of God" coming to earth. (Fun fact: Matthew usually has Jesus talking about the "kingdom of heaven," while the other gospels say "the kingdom of God." That's not a theological difference—it's a cultural one. Out of reverence, many Jews avoided saying God's name directly, using "heaven" as a respectful stand-in.[1] Same kingdom. Same idea.) But let's be real—that concept can be confusing. And Jesus didn't make it simpler by using metaphors:

"The kingdom of heaven is like a mustard seed" (Matthew 13:31).

"The kingdom of heaven is like a merchant looking for fine pearls" (Matthew 13:45).

It all seems a little cryptic. But that's because Jesus was speaking in the rich, layered language of Jewish tradition. He wasn't starting a brand-new conversation; he was stepping into one that had already been going on for generations. The concept of the "kingdom of heaven" reflects the Jewish expression *malkut shamayim*, which literally means "rule of heaven." It's a phrase that refers to God's dynamic reign.[2] Here, Jesus is talking about God's rule and reign on planet earth—right here, right now.

Dallas Willard defines God's kingdom as the "range of his effective will"[3]—the place where what God wants done is actually done. The idea is that wherever God's will is being done, his kingdom is present and on display. It can look like this:

When people love their neighbors, the kingdom of heaven is on display.
When husbands care for their sick wives, the kingdom of heaven is on display.
When children honor their parents, the kingdom of heaven is on display.
When parents love their children tenderly, the kingdom of heaven is on display.
When governments take care of the most vulnerable, the kingdom of heaven is on display.
When businesspeople use their money to facilitate kingdom work, the kingdom of heaven is on display.

But here's the crazy part: It seems that one of the very places in the entire universe where God's will isn't automatically done is here, on earth. In human hearts. Willard puts it this way: "Indeed, the social and political realm, along with the individual heart, is the only place in all of creation where the kingdom of God, or his effective will, is currently permitted to be absent."[4]

That's why Jesus teaches us to pray, "Your kingdom come, your will be done, on earth as it is in heaven." He's not asking us to pray the kingdom into existence. It already exists. He's inviting us to welcome it, to let it take over the places where it's been shut out. When Jesus preached, his message wasn't "Hey, the kingdom is finally here." It was "The kingdom is now accessible." He wants us to step into it—right now—through him.

When we pray this phrase, we're daring greatly! We're inviting God's rule to extend into real, public life: the visible, social, relational, and political spaces of the world. And so what we pray every time we say this part of the Lord's Prayer is essentially this: "Father, let what is true in heaven become true here—in my life, in my home, in my city."

And that sounds lovely . . . until God's kingdom starts to conflict with ours. Because here's the truth: We each have our own little kingdom—and we want to rule it, unobstructed.[5] Your "kingdom" is the space in your life where you exercise full control, where whatever you say goes. It's the little world where you are king. And this instinct kicks in early. Several years ago I was outside playing soccer with one of my boys, Jack—he was six at the time. He'd just started playing Minecraft, and mid-dribble he casually told me about a dream he had.

"Dad," he said, "all the girls in the world were trying to kiss me. And if they did, I was gonna turn into a ghast." (For the uninitiated: In Minecraft, ghasts are massive, floating jellyfish-ghosts that shoot explosive fireballs. Terrifying.)

WE'RE INVITING
GOD'S RULE TO
EXTEND INTO REAL,
PUBLIC LIFE: THE
VISIBLE, SOCIAL,
RELATIONAL, AND
POLITICAL SPACES
OF THE WORLD.

So I asked, "What happened?"

He said, "I built a portal and disappeared into the Nether. And in the Nether, they couldn't kiss me. They had to choose—serve me or die."

I was starting to get nervous about the mindset of this child who shares half my DNA. I pressed on. "Interesting," I said. "Is this a world you created in your mind? Do you go there often?"

He replied, "Nah, it was just a Minecraft dream. But it was amazing."

I followed up with, "Just out of curiosity, would you ever kiss a girl on the lips?"

Without hesitation he said, "I'm *never* gonna kiss a girl on the lips."

"Good lad," I said. "Let's shake on that."

Now, why do I tell you this story? Because in his own hilarious, Minecraft-y way, my son was dreaming about building a kingdom, a place where everything went exactly the way he wanted. Where he held all the power. Where the world bent to his will. It's adorable . . . but also relatable.

So let me ask you this: What are your kingdom fantasies? If you were in charge of everything—if your kingdom came—what would that look like?

Here's my guess:

You'd probably have more money.

A bigger house.

Better friends—who never bring drama.

If you're single, maybe your dream partner would be wildly attractive, immensely kind, exceedingly rich—and perfectly aligned with all your hopes and dreams (even the irresponsible ones). No conflict. No chaos. No challenge.

If your ultimate desires shaped your actual world, your kingdom would look very different from your current life. So would mine. In the kingdom of Matt Smallbone, there would be a pool in the backyard. I'd eat at fancy restaurants all the time. I'd have enough money to fly my whole family to Australia every year. Also, there would be rules about hard conversations. You could have them only during designated hours. And only once a month. Oh, and there would be unlimited ice cream.

My kingdom would be *awesome*. The only problem is that I would be in charge of all things. And it would be a pretty shallow existence for my minions. (Though the dessert game would be strong.)

So you should thank God—literally—that my kingdom doesn't define your reality. Because the values of my kingdom don't hold a candle to the values of God's. Because while the values of my kingdom might seem pretty great for me, Jesus made a bold claim: His kingdom is good news—for everyone.

Mark captures Jesus's words like this: "The kingdom of God has come near. Repent and believe the good news!" (Mark 1:15). But what exactly is the good news of the kingdom of God? To really get it, we have to rewind all the way back to the beginning of Scripture. In Genesis 1 and 2, we see a world where everything is beautifully aligned: Relationships are whole, creation is in sync, minds and souls are at peace. Why? Because God is King.[6] His reign is uncontested. His kingdom shapes everything. Life works because his rule leads the way.

But then in Genesis 3, the story turns. Humanity decides to

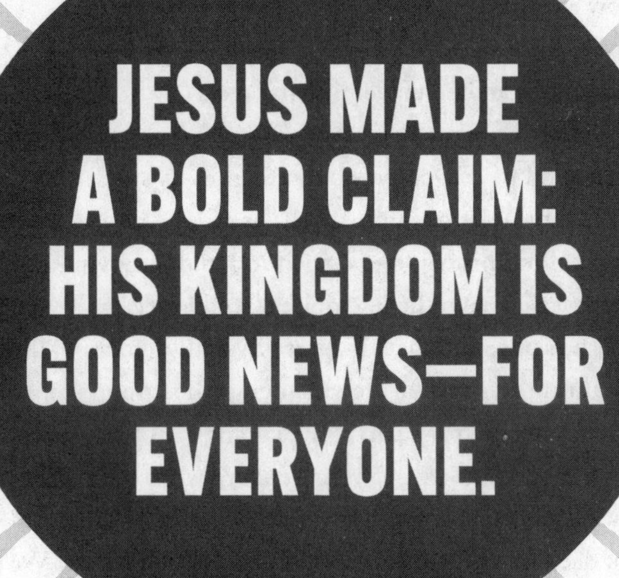
JESUS MADE
A BOLD CLAIM:
HIS KINGDOM IS
GOOD NEWS—FOR
EVERYONE.

go off script, to crown ourselves kings and queens and run the show our own way. That decision fractures everything. Because when we make life all about us, things inevitably fall apart. And nothing makes life more miserable (or more boring) than being obsessed with ourselves.

Ever wonder why there's war? Or political division? Or why families implode? At the root, it's the same old problem: me at the center.

How am I doing?

How do I look?

Why didn't more people like that reel?

Am I getting what I deserve?

That kind of self-preoccupation leaves us stuck and disconnected. It ruins relationships. It robs us of joy.

Throughout history, we've tried to build our own kingdoms, reigning over our own little empires. And every single time, the result is the same: Things fall apart physically, emotionally, spiritually, culturally. It's like we're dancing the wrong steps to the wrong song at the wrong party. Like doing the electric slide backward . . . in 3/4 time . . . at your cousin's wedding. Everything's out of sync.

But deep down, humans long to get back in rhythm. We crave harmony with the way the world was meant to be. That longing echoes through every culture's stories. Different characters, same theme: A true King will return, defeat the dragon, wake the sleepers, free the captives, and lead us back to the life we were made for.

And that, Jesus says, is the good news of the kingdom:

The true King has come.

And he's setting things right again.

When we bring our lives under Jesus's wise and loving rule, life begins to work properly again. Not perfectly—but better. Like a child flourishing under the care of a good parent. Or a team thriving under a great coach.

And so Jesus tells us to pray that his kingdom would come, that his rule would shape the way the world works.

So when we pray, "Your kingdom come," we're asking Jesus to reign—

In our homes.

On our streets.

In our politics.

In our schools.

In our churches.

In our conversations over coffee.

And deep in our hearts.

This kind of prayer has a name: *intercessory prayer.* Pete Greig puts it simply: "Intercessory prayer is asking God for the needs of other people or other situations."[7] In biblical terms, intercession means partnering with God to see his kingdom come—right here, right now. Notice that when Jesus teaches us to pray, "Your kingdom come," he's implying that God's kingdom hasn't fully arrived yet. Not everywhere. Not in every heart. Not in every situation. Here's the radical idea: Jesus shows us that through prayer we can participate in bending reality toward our Father's good intentions.

But some of us aren't convinced that prayer actually does anything. I get it. I've been there. For a good stretch in my late twenties and early thirties, I didn't pray much at all. It felt like

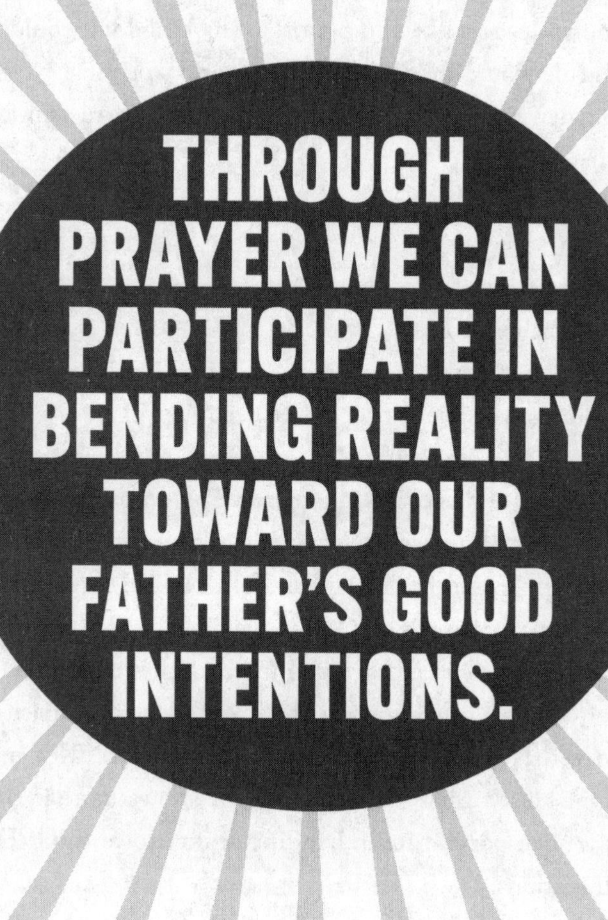
THROUGH
PRAYER WE CAN
PARTICIPATE IN
BENDING REALITY
TOWARD OUR
FATHER'S GOOD
INTENTIONS.

a waste of time. And then I came across this gem from Dallas Willard, who—as you can tell by now—has played a significant role in my spiritual growth:

> God's response to our prayers is not a charade. He does not pretend that He is answering our prayers when He is only doing what He was going to do anyway. Our requests really do make a difference in what God does or does not do. The idea that everything would happen exactly as it does, regardless of whether we pray or not, is a specter that haunts the minds of many who sincerely profess belief in God. It makes prayer psychologically impossible, replacing it with dead ritual at best. And, of course, God does not respond to this. You wouldn't either.[8]

Today I hope you sense the invitation to dare greatly, to step into intercessory prayer—not as a ritual but as a world-changing partnership with God.

So how do we do that?

I offer you four simple steps from Pete Greig:[9]

1. GET INFORMED

You can't pray with power about things you don't understand. Whether it's a neighbor, a city, a country, or a conflict, do your homework. The more you learn, the more specific, wise, and passionate your prayers will become.

2. GET INSPIRED

Intercession isn't just about asking God to fix stuff. It's about aligning our hearts with his.

Ask, "What does God want to do here? What is he showing me, through Scripture, through his Spirit, through the needs around me?" Listen. He'll let you know. Then let that holy imagination shape how you pray.

3. GET INDIGNANT

The things that break God's heart should break ours too. Intercession is a passionate act. It's bold. It's disruptive. When we intercede, we aren't just feeling sorry for the brokenness; we're engaging with it. We believe God can bring change, and through prayer we partner with him to bring that change into being.

4. GET IN SYNC

There's power in praying together. Always has been. Find people who want to see God move, and start praying with them. When we unite in prayer around shared burdens, something shifts. Heaven listens. Earth shakes. God's kingdom comes.

Let's pray like Jesus told us to. It matters!

PRACTICAL PRAYER TIPS

Set aside at least five minutes to practice intercessory prayer by praying, "Your kingdom come."

Before you do anything else, slow down.

Take a deep breath.

Recognize that you're in the presence of the King who has a clear mandate on how things should run on planet earth.

Now pray the Lord's Prayer out loud—not quickly, not mechanically, but slowly and reverently:

> Our Father in heaven,
> hallowed be your name,
> *your kingdom come,*
> your will be done,
>   on earth as it is in heaven.
> Give us today our daily bread.
> And forgive us our debts,
>   as we also have forgiven our debtors.
> And lead us not into temptation,
>   but deliver us from the evil one.

Then pause.

Go back and linger over this phrase: "your kingdom come."

Take a few moments to ask yourself:

- Where in my life does God's rule still feel distant?
- Where—in my heart, home, school, relationships, city—is Jesus not yet King?

Now put Greig's four simple steps into practice:

GET INFORMED

Think of a situation in your city or in the world that desperately needs the kingdom of God: homelessness, addiction, injustice, isolation, division.

Name it.

GET INSPIRED

Ask: What would it look like if God's rule showed up there?

Visualize it. Let your imagination paint a better picture.

GET INDIGNANT

Let a holy discontent rise up in you.

Ask: Why does this matter to God? What needs to change?

Let that conviction fuel your prayer.

GET IN SYNC

Don't do this alone.

Share the burden with friends. Ask them to pray with you.

Partner with people, and with heaven, until breakthrough comes.

You might even pray something like this:

Jesus, I want your kingdom to come—in me, around me, and through me. Help me let go of my agenda. Let your rule begin in my heart. Bring your peace where there is conflict, your healing where there is pain, your

beauty where there is chaos. May your kingdom come,
here and now.

And then sit in silence.

Be still.

Listen.

Note what you're hearing. Write it down.

And finally, if you're ready to go all in, tell your heavenly Father that you submit to his rule and reign in your life.

WHEN THE FATHER'S PLAN IS BEST

"Our Father in heaven,
hallowed be your name,
your kingdom come,
your will be done,
on earth as it is in heaven."

—MATTHEW 6:9–10, EMPHASIS ADDED

When we pray, we ought to trust that God, like a loving father, is much wiser than we are and that in the end he does what he knows is best.

—JOHN M. FRAME

As I mentioned earlier, in a former life I was a professional musician. I had the privilege of touring as a bass player for several Christian artists. It was a good life—fun, full of purpose, and built around music and worship. I was on the road in 2010 with the incredibly gifted (and kind) Michael W. Smith. We were wrapping up a West Coast tour—just one final show in California before heading home. It had been a two-week run, and I hadn't seen my young family in a while. Mary was back in Nashville, holding down the fort with our three boys—all under the age of five. And just before I had left, we found out that baby number four was on the way. We were going to need a minivan.

Now, here's a little rule of thumb for anyone traveling while their pregnant wife and three toddlers are at home: Never put your phone on silent. But on this particular day, after we had played late into the night, I was exhausted. So I switched my phone to "Do Not Disturb" to get a bit of much-needed shut-eye. At 10:00 a.m. Pacific time, I woke up in my hotel suite and reached for my phone only to see that I had several missed calls and messages from Mary. There were two texts I'll never forget:

> 7:03 a.m.—"Babe, I'm bleeding. Can you call?"
> 9:17 a.m.—"I'm heading to the doctor."

My heart sank. And then fear took over. I started praying with a kind of desperation I hadn't known before, pleading with God to save the life of our unborn child. I invoked the name of Jesus. I summoned every scrap of faith I had.

Then came the next message: "We've lost the baby."

I remember staring at the screen, stunned. And then I got angry. Really angry. I had it out with God: "This is incredibly unfair! I've given my life to serving you. I've led people in worship around the world. And this is how you repay me?"

The cruelest part? By the time I made it home the next morning, everything was already over: the appointments, the medical details, the loss. Mary had gone through all of it alone. On the other side of the world from her own parents. Without me. I wasn't there to hold her, or cry with her, or carry any of the pain.

To say I was disappointed with God would be an understatement. We lost a baby I hadn't even had time to fully celebrate yet. I felt shame. I felt grief. I felt guilt. But mostly I was furious. And for a long time after that, I stopped praying. What was the point? Sure, I still believed God existed. But I figured he must be pretty disconnected, too distant to care about the small stuff that the little people like me are crying out for.

It launched me into a theological crisis: If God really hears our prayers, what happened here? I wrestled with the words of Jesus, especially in John 14–17 in what's known as the Farewell Discourse. Jesus makes some pretty astonishing promises about prayer:

> I will do whatever you ask in my name, so that the Father may be glorified in the Son. You may ask me for anything in my name, and I will do it. (John 14:13–14)

> If you remain in me and my words remain in you, ask whatever you wish, and it will be done for you. (John 15:7)

> You did not choose me, but I chose you . . . so that whatever you ask in my name the Father will give you. (John 15:16)

> In that day you will no longer ask me anything. Very truly I tell you, my Father will give you whatever you ask in my name. . . . Ask and you will receive, and your joy will be complete. (John 16:23–24)

That's five times in one sitting that Jesus looks his disciples in the eyes and says, "Ask anything in my name, and I'll do it."

I remember thinking, "Really, Jesus? Anything? Because we *did* ask in your name. And our baby still died. What am I missing?"

Now, the easy answer is that much of what we pray for isn't technically "in Jesus's name." "In Jesus's name" was never meant to be a magic phrase we tack onto the end of a prayer to get what we want.[1] In the first century, a person's name was synonymous with their nature. So when Jesus said to pray in his name, he meant that our prayers should be in alignment with his character—his heart, his mission, his values.[2]

To pray in Jesus's name is to pray for the things Jesus would pray for. It's to ask for what he wants. To desire what he desires. That's why, despite my best teenage efforts, God never answered my heartfelt prayers to be incredibly wealthy, world-famous, and impossibly good-looking (still waiting on the first two!). I joke. But the truth is, when we use the biblical definition, a lot of what we pray for isn't actually in Jesus's name. And I think that explains a huge portion of unanswered prayer. Honestly? Probably about 99 percent.

But that still leaves 1 percent, doesn't it? And that 1 percent has caused me considerable angst over the years—because what about the prayers that are aligned with what I understand about

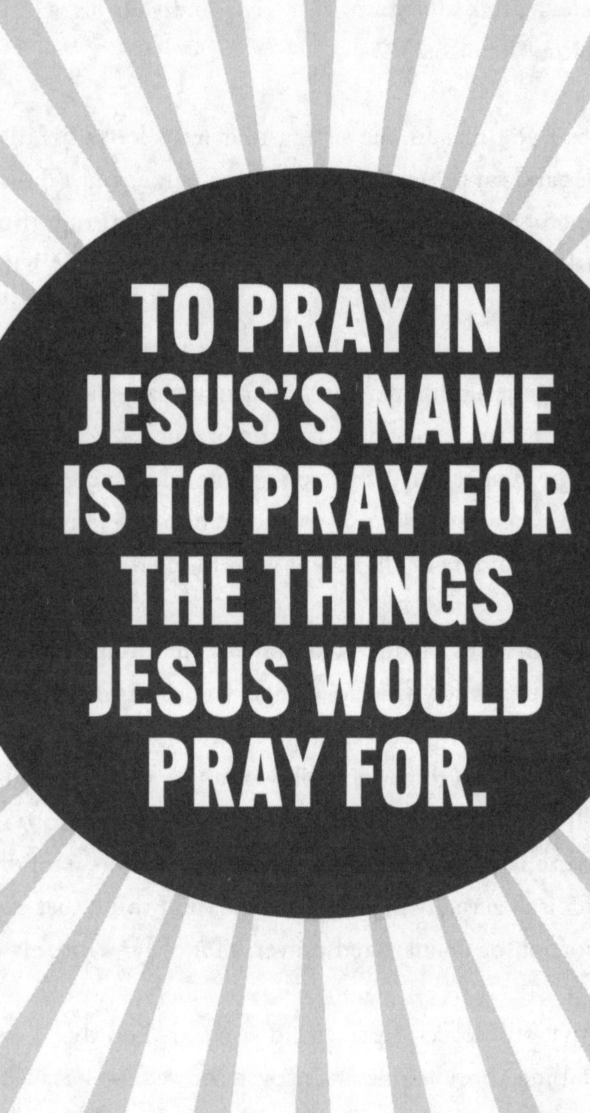
TO PRAY IN
JESUS'S NAME
IS TO PRAY FOR
THE THINGS
JESUS WOULD
PRAY FOR.

his nature? Like the healing of a child. Or the restoration of a marriage. Or freedom from addiction. What about those? Why aren't those always answered?*

One thing I'm learning as I pray this part of the Lord's Prayer every day is that some prayers aren't answered because my motives are off. James, Jesus's little brother, put it bluntly: "When you ask, you do not receive, because you ask with wrong motives, that you may spend what you get on your pleasures" (James 4:3). It turns out, Jesus never promised to answer every prayer just because we ask. What truly matters for the issue at hand is that we start our prayer petitions by prioritizing God's motives over our own—as best we can discern them.

A second reason some prayers go unanswered? Because God himself is the better answer. Sometimes he allows the ache to linger. Not because he doesn't care but because he wants to draw us closer to him.

Thirdly, some prayers aren't answered because of free will. Just because we pray for someone to stop drinking doesn't mean God will remove their capacity to make their own choices about their personal alcohol consumption. God is not a bully. He doesn't force people to obey him against their will. He's a humble king. And if we don't understand that, we'll keep being confused about unanswered prayer. Could God override human decisions? Sure. But usually he honors the agency he gave us, something Blaise Pascal called "the dignity of causality."[3] God isn't a puppet master pulling every string. He's not trying to manipulate us into

* I'm grateful to Pete Greig's research in his incredibly helpful book *God on Mute*, which contributed heavily to this chapter.

compliance. He's a Father who invites, who loves, who listens, and who lets us choose.

And that's why prayer isn't about bending God to our will. It's about aligning our hearts with his. It's about asking that the things he's always cared about—peace, healing, forgiveness, justice, beauty—would take root in the real world. In our world. Just as they are in heaven!

Ultimately, the main reason prayers go unanswered? Pete Greig suggests that it's because our prayers are not in line with God's will.[4] And this brings us right back to the line we're focusing on here in the Lord's Prayer. When Jesus taught his disciples to pray, he insisted they start by aligning their will with the Father's: "Your will be done, on earth as it is in heaven."

This means sometimes we pray prayers that go against God's will. And in his love for us, he says no. This part of the Lord's Prayer is all about how God's will interacts with human free will to shape what happens in our lives. Yes, it's a bit of a mind-bender. The tension between God's sovereignty and our freedom is one of the great mysteries of faith. We may never fully resolve it. And that's okay. Because when you're dealing with a higher consciousness, some mystery is just part of the package.

Let me try to explain it this way: Our little rescue pup, Rosie, decided years ago that I'm her king. She looks at me with those big, desperate eyes that say, "Hey, King, how about tossing a slice of that pizza off the counter for your girl?" She wants to be near me. She follows me around. And honestly, she kind of worships me. In biblical terms you could say she abides in me. She loves me, and I love her. But there are things about my world—my "kingdom"—that she just can't understand. She gets sad when I leave the house.

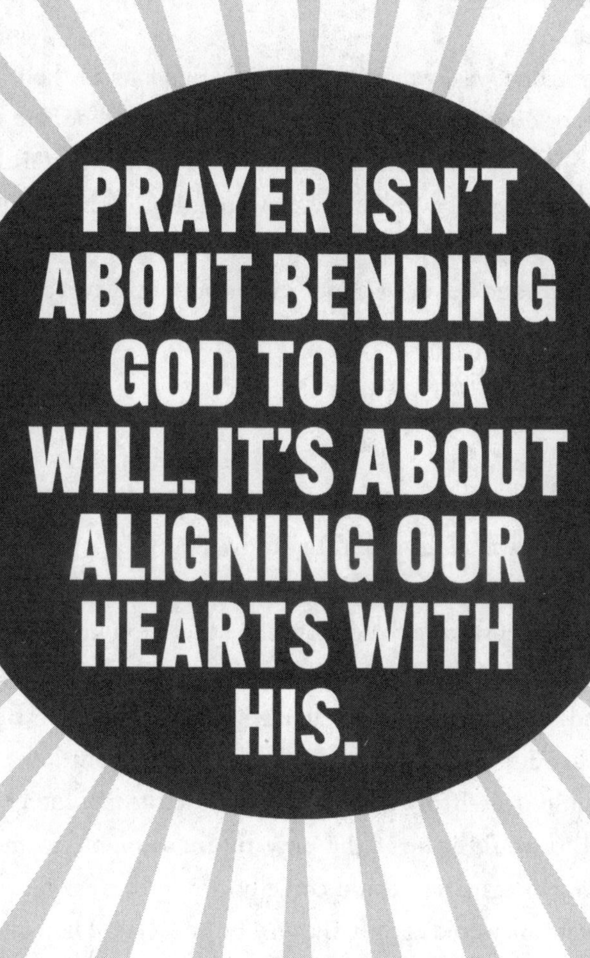
PRAYER ISN'T
ABOUT BENDING
GOD TO OUR
WILL. IT'S ABOUT
ALIGNING OUR
HEARTS WITH
HIS.

What she doesn't know is that I have to leave the house to pay for the house. She wants me home 24/7. But she has no concept of work or mortgages or insurance premiums. I'm sure she has all kinds of questions about where I go for so long. But here's the thing: She is still safe, loved, and cared for, even in all her confusion.

In the same way, we may never fully understand the reasons God does or doesn't do something. But we can still be safe in his love, even with our questions. Looking back, I'm grateful that many of my prayers haven't been answered. If God had answered all my early prayers, I'd be divorced from Madonna and touring with a circus. And not even a good circus but a midlevel one where the elephants look sad. The fact that I'm not is evidence enough of divine intervention.

Instead, I'm very happily married to Mary (but still working in a circus).

P. T. Forsyth put it like this: "We shall come one day to a heaven where we shall gratefully know that God's great refusals were sometimes the true answers to our truest prayers."[5] Sometimes we just have to acknowledge that God knows best.

This knowledge that God knows best is the only thing that has dulled the ache of our miscarriage. It's still a wound. But I'm slowly learning to trust that God's "no" came from love. How tragic would it be if my destiny were limited to my logic? How small a life would it be if the only future available to me was the one my imagination could come up with? If every one of my prayers were answered exactly the way I wanted—if I had ultimate power over the universe—I don't think I'd become a better man. I think I'd become narrower, more selfish, more lost.

That's why it's really good news that we don't run the world. There's a God who governs human history with wisdom, compassion, and a long view. Isaiah 55:9 reminds us,

> As the heavens are higher than the earth,
> so are my ways higher than your ways
> and my thoughts than your thoughts.

Now when I look at Mary and our four kids, I just have to believe God said no back then to my prayer for our unborn baby for reasons that are good for us, that I simply lack the intelligence to understand. Nothing about miscarriage seems fair, but as I have walked this painful path, I have concluded that he's still good even if I never get a clear answer to my "why." These days—fifteen years later—I am at peace.

Another area where I've struggled to submit to God's will is my professional life. As a teenager, my career goals were clear:

1. Become a professional cricketer and/or basketballer or
2. Become a rock star.

Either would have been fine because I was committed to having fun as an adult, and I figured these "jobs" would make me a pile of cash. Pastoring? That sounded like voluntarily signing up for a lifetime of misery. So I should probably confess something: I never set out to be a pastor. If you had told my twenty-five-year-old self that I'd one day be leading a church, I would've laughed right in your smug Christian face.

But God's will has a way of rerouting us in ways we don't

see coming. And one of my favorite examples of that in my own life began with, of all things, a mango smoothie. One random Tuesday, my cousin Josh, who was still in high school at the time, decided he was thirsty. Not just thirsty—mango smoothie thirsty. He walked into a local coffee shop in Franklin, Tennessee, placed his order, and noticed the barista. For reasons he still can't fully explain, he did something out of character: He asked for her number.

Meanwhile, Mary and I were living in Columbia, Tennessee, with three young boys, and I was wrapping up my touring career as a bass player. Around that time, the new worship leader at our church asked me to play in the band. Fast-forward a few years and that friendship led me to my first ministry role at a church in Florida. I loved it there. The ocean was a block from our offices, and I could surf at lunch. We literally had "board meetings." Things were humming along nicely. The surfer church grew so fast we had to add a fourth service, which meant adding one on Saturday night. One result of this was that the senior pastor couldn't officiate Saturday evening weddings anymore.

Guess who had no preaching responsibilities, an interesting accent, and an open weekend calendar. Yep, your boy was now the official wedding guy. And for a few years, I officiated *tons* of weddings. It taught me two things: Love is sacred, and people will spend a small fortune to ensure their dog is part of the ceremony. Because of Salty Church's thriving young adults ministry, I did a serious number of weddings and became good at officiating them. I had that thirty-minute wedding ceremony down to a tight set. It was *Seinfeld* meets Song of Songs.

Then came the summer of 2014. Cousin Josh—the mango

smoothie guy—asked me to officiate his wedding to that barista who we finally learned was named Emily. It was at a beautiful outdoor venue just south of Franklin. And, folks, the feedback was that I crushed it. Afterward, this Aussie guy by the name of Darren Whitehead walked up and said, "Mate! We just started a new church called Church of the City, and we're going to need a lead pastor for a campus in Nashville. Would you be open to talking about it?"

I gave him the most honest answer I could: "That's very kind, but there's a slight issue. I don't really know how to preach. I haven't had much opportunity."

He just smiled and said, "I dunno, man. I think we could help you with that."

And that's how—through a mango smoothie, a change in church service times, a wedding gig, and an openness to letting God's will be done despite my intended career path—I ended up in my dream role, pastoring in the city I love.

When I look back at that whole chain of events, I can see now what I couldn't see then: Heaven was quietly invading my little patch of earth. None of it looked spiritual or strategic at the time. It looked like errands and scheduling conflicts and ordinary Tuesdays. But this is how God's will usually works its way into our lives—not as a dramatic plot twist but as a quiet rerouting that makes sense only in hindsight.

That's why Jesus teaches us to pray, "Your will be done, on earth as it is in heaven." Not because we're surrendering to fate but because we're learning to trust that God is weaving heaven's wisdom into the ordinary moments of our story. When we pray these words, we're saying, "Father, take the small stuff—my coffee shop moments, my calendar, my plans—and make them conduits for something I can't yet see." The mango smoothie wasn't the point. The point was learning to release the steering wheel and trust that God knows the road better than I do.

PRACTICAL PRAYER TIPS

I invite you to spend at least five minutes surrendering to the will of God in prayer. Start by slowing down. Take a deep breath. Place both feet on the floor, open your hands, and simply say, "Here I am, God."

Now pray the full Lord's Prayer aloud—slowly, thoughtfully, intentionally:

> Our Father in heaven,
> hallowed be your name,
> your kingdom come,
> *your will be done,*
> *on earth as it is in heaven.*
> Give us today our daily bread.
> And forgive us our debts,
> as we also have forgiven our debtors.
> And lead us not into temptation,
> but deliver us from the evil one.

Now return to this phrase: "your will be done, on earth as it is in heaven."

Sit with it.

Let it speak to your heart.

Let it search you.

Ask honestly, "God, is anything in my life out of alignment with your will? Is there something I've been grasping for, something I've been trying to control, that I need to surrender?"

Here's a prayer to help you put words to your surrender:

Father, I want your will more than mine. Even when I don't understand, I trust that your plans are wiser and kinder than my own.

So I surrender my timing, my desires, my expectations, and I say, "Your will be done."

In me. Through me. Around me.

Then just be still for a moment.

Breathe.

Listen.

Let surrender do its quiet, deep work in your soul.

And if you're in a private space, go ahead and raise your hands in the air. Not out of emotion or hype but as a humble posture of surrender.

SEVEN

THE GREAT ADVENTURE OF DAILY BREAD

"Our Father in heaven,
hallowed be your name,
your kingdom come,
your will be done,
on earth as it is in heaven.
Give us today our daily bread."

—MATTHEW 6:9–11, EMPHASIS ADDED

There's always that: today's bread is enough bread, today's grace is enough grace, today's God is enough God.

—ANN VOSKAMP

It was the fall of 2007, and Mary and I had just welcomed our second child, Caleb, into the world. We had been living in the

United States for about eighteen months, and let me tell you, this whole first-generation immigrant thing is no joke. Our household income fluctuated between $150 and $300 a week. Because of my visa restrictions, I could only earn money through the Aussie band I was in, and even that was hit-or-miss.

In fact, Caleb's entire hospital stay was covered by the state of Tennessee. I remember feeling a strange shame about that. I tried to pay something, and the hospital staff basically said, "You don't have any money, sir. It's okay. This one's on us. Use what you have to take care of your family."

We were living off homemade pancakes. We attended any church event that served food. To say we were just scraping by might be the understatement of the century. That fall, our band's checking account was worryingly low. And then our lead singer started losing her voice—constantly. We had to cancel a bunch of shows. Shortly after Caleb was born, we hit a stretch of weeks with no income at all. I remember multiple days when it was genuinely unclear how we would feed our family.

And that was when I began to learn the power of praying for "our daily bread." This kind of prayer is called petitionary prayer. Petitionary prayer is when we ask God for something. These requests are usually where people *start* in prayer. But not Jesus. As we have seen through the previous chapters, Jesus would first adore the Father and submit to his will. Only after that would he ask for stuff.

Personally, I didn't learn petitionary prayer from a theology book. I learned it from desperation. We needed God to show up—and he did. That year, Mary and I experienced miracle after miracle. A few times food showed up on our front porch. To this day, we have no idea who left it there. Other days someone would invite us to dinner last minute, no explanation. God was literally giving us our daily bread. And that's exactly what Jesus told us to ask for.

So just a quick reminder before we dive into this section: The Lord's Prayer moves in six distinct parts—six movements, like verses in a song. The first half orients us toward *God*—you'll notice all the "your" language: *your* name, *your* kingdom, *your* will. Then the second half shifts to *us*—our needs, our struggles, our dependence. This structure is not random. Jesus is showing us the order of a healthy prayer life: Start by centering on who God is before moving to what we need.

So far we've been focused on the first half—on God's character, his holiness, his nearness, and his desire for his kingdom to take root right here on planet earth (and in our hearts). Before we ever get to *our* requests, Jesus wants us to pause and remember who we're talking to.

God is not a distant deity.

He's not a vending machine for spiritual favors.

He's a *Father.*

And not just any father—a Father who's as close as the air we breathe.

A Father who is holy, who is good, and who can be trusted.

A Father whose ways we want to see come to life right here, right now—in our city, in our family, in our church.

A Father whose will is better than our own, even when that's hard to swallow.

That's the foundation. That's where we've been so far in this prayer Jesus is teaching us.

But now Jesus shifts gears. Now we move inward. Now we talk about our needs. Jesus says, If you have a need, ask. Don't overcomplicate it. Just ask. He starts with this line: "Give us today our daily bread" (Matthew 6:11). It's a strange little phrase in English, isn't it? You'd never say, "Give me *today* my *daily*" anything. For example, no one says, "Give me today my daily clean socks, Mother!" It sounds redundant.

So pay attention: Whenever the Bible sounds a bit odd in English, that's usually a sign that something interesting is happening in the original language—something we don't want to miss. And as we're about to see, hidden in these few simple words is a whole theology of dependence, trust, and provision. Jesus is teaching us how to live *one* day at a time.

The first thing we need to pay attention to in this short phrase is that Jesus tells us to pray for "us" and "our," not "me" and "mine."

Give *us* today *our* daily bread.

We need to stop and confess something here: As a culture, we are much better at "me and mine" than "us and our." Many thinkers like theologian Carl Trueman have pointed out that Western culture has been shaped by a deep, often unquestioned "expressive individualism."[1] Meaning that the gravitational pull of our world is toward making the self the center of everything. And without even realizing it, we start to see our lives primarily through the lens of our needs, our desires, and our story, instead of the common good we're called to pursue together.

When we read this prayer, we often misread it. We make it individual. We center ourselves right in the middle of the narrative. But Jesus is teaching us to pray in community—with and for each other. This kind of prayer assumes we will share what we receive, not hoard it.

A beautiful story from Mother Teresa's letters illustrates this beautifully:

> I will never forget the night an old gentleman came to our house and said that there was a family with eight children and they had not eaten, and could we do something for them. So I took some rice and went there. The mother took the rice from my hands, then she divided it into two and went out. I could see the faces of the children shining with hunger. When she came back, I asked her where she had gone. She gave me a very simple answer: "They are hungry also." And "they" were the family next door and she knew that they were hungry.[2]

In this mother's mind, there was no such thing as "my rice," only "our rice." Even when her own children were hungry. She understood the power of "our daily bread."

So let's talk about "daily bread." The Greek word Jesus uses for "daily" here is *epiousios*—a rare and tricky little word. Many scholars note that it doesn't show up anywhere else in ancient Greek literature.[3] Most English Bible translations go with "daily," but the word may carry deeper meaning. Some scholars think it means "necessary for life" or "substantial," highlighting bread as the essential thing that sustains us.[4] Others argue it means "bread for the future"—a prayer for not just today's needs but also tomorrow's trust. Whatever the nuance, the heart of the prayer is clear:

We are to ask for God's sustaining provision, whether it's food for today, grace for tomorrow, or strength for the road ahead.

So why bread? Why not daily steak or daily truffle risotto? Well, while Matthew wrote in Greek, he was raised Jewish, and to the Jewish mind the Hebrew word *lehem* doesn't just mean bread. It's shorthand for food in general.[5] So "daily bread" isn't just about gluten; it's about all kinds of provision. When we pray for daily bread, we're asking God to provide for all our needs—big and small—for ourselves, our families, and our communities. And it's not just physical needs. Tim Keller writes, "Praying for our 'daily bread' for ourselves should cover the full range of what we need spiritually, emotionally, and materially."[6]

Jesus's prayer for "daily bread" speaks to our psychological needs too. Because some of us carry real anxiety that we won't have enough. We may be okay today, but what about tomorrow? What if the paycheck doesn't come? What if the fridge breaks? What if the car won't start? How will we make it?

This deep fear of not having enough to eat can mess with those of us who have felt the shame of not being able to buy everything that we put in our grocery cart, or who regularly rely on help from external sources to not be hungry. Jesus meets us there.

When we pray for daily bread, we're not just asking for food. We're praying for deliverance from the fear that there won't be enough. And that's the invitation: to trust that our Father knows what we need and will provide it. It's the same kind of trust little kids have when they look at Mum and Dad and say, "They've got this. I don't need to worry." That's what Jesus is teaching us. That's the kind of trust that frees us from anxiety.

Maybe you already know this because you've lived it. You've

WHEN WE
PRAY FOR DAILY
BREAD, WE'RE ASKING
GOD TO PROVIDE FOR ALL
OUR NEEDS—BIG AND
SMALL—FOR OURSELVES,
OUR FAMILIES,
AND OUR
COMMUNITIES.

walked through hard seasons and seen God show up. You've prayed this prayer out of necessity, not theory. And now you carry that calm, nonanxious presence that comes only from having experienced God's faithfulness.

Others of us? We're still figuring this out. We've never been that desperate. We've never needed to ask God for literal bread because there's always been food on the table and money in the account. And because of that, we don't really have a clue about how to ask for what we need.

It's almost as if Jesus anticipated this. Because in Luke's version of the Lord's Prayer, he follows it with a story, a parable about asking for bread: "Then Jesus said to them, 'Suppose you have a friend, and you go to him at midnight and say, "Friend, lend me three loaves of bread"'" (Luke 11:5).

Jesus is telling this story to make an important point. In this little parable, he wants you to picture yourself as the world's most annoying, presumptuous, and poorly organized neighbor. The clock has just struck midnight. Everyone is asleep. The neighborhood is dark and still. And there you are, knocking on the door of your buddy's house—who, by the way, just got his newborn to sleep. You're standing there, whisper-shouting through the door, trying not to wake the baby, and you say, "A friend of mine on a journey has come to me, and I have no food to offer him" (Luke 11:6).

It's important to understand that in that time and place, hospitality wasn't optional—it was a duty. A visitor was to be welcomed and fed, regardless of the time of their arrival.[7] Having nothing to serve a guest wasn't just inconvenient; it was deeply shameful. You were expected to show honor through generosity.

So you can feel this guy's panic. He's embarrassed. He's desperate. When Jesus tells the story, we're supposed to feel that tension. He wants us to imagine that moment of awkwardness, where you're caught without what you need and you have to rely on someone else's kindness to save face.

The story continues: "And suppose the one inside answers, 'Don't bother me. The door is already locked, and my children and I are in bed. I can't get up and give you anything'" (Luke 11:7).

Homes back then were small—one room, maybe two. Everyone would've been sleeping side by side on the floor.[8] So if Dad got up, everyone got up. This wasn't just inconvenient; it was chaos. The kids would start crying, the baby would start screaming—total disaster. No wonder the guy inside said, "Don't bother me." But still, the friend outside was stuck. He needed help. And even though it was late, the man inside felt some cultural pressure to come through.

And then Jesus, in full storyteller mode, drops the punch line: "I tell you, even though he will not get up and give you the bread because of friendship, yet because of your shameless audacity he will surely get up and give you as much as you need" (Luke 11:8).

I love that phrase—*shameless audacity*. It's one of those moments when Jesus gives us a window into the kind of bold, persistent posture he wants in prayer. And notice that now we have two relational metaphors at work: God as Father and God as Friend. There's something beautiful about that mix. As a dad myself, I get it. My kids can come to me confidently because I'm their dad. They know I love them. And also, it's kind of in the father job description to help out your kiddos. But there is also a friend component as they age. I'm happy to help them because I like them, not just because I *have* to. Here, Jesus is saying that's what God is like when we ask for stuff. He's both a great father and friend.

And then Jesus goes further, explaining what this shameless audacity looks like in real life: "So I say to you: Ask and it will be given to you; seek and you will find; knock and the door will be opened to you. For everyone who asks receives; the one who seeks finds; and to the one who knocks, the door will be opened" (Luke 11:9–10). Notice the three action words there: *ask*, *seek*, and *knock*. In the original Greek, they're written in the continuous present tense, which means we're not to ask just once but to *keep on asking*. Not knock and walk away, but *keep on knocking*.[9] In other words, Jesus is saying, "Don't give up. Keep coming. Keep asking. Keep believing."

This is a *wild* twist. Because at first glance, it almost sounds like Jesus is comparing God to a grumpy "get off my grass" neighbor who doesn't want to help you. And if you just annoy him long enough, he'll finally cave in and give you what you want. But that's not what Jesus is teaching at all. The point here is that prayer isn't meant to be passive. It's not a "pray once and forget about it" kind of deal. It's persistent. It's expectant. It's relational.

According to Jesus, persistence in prayer matters. Keep asking. Keep seeking. Keep knocking. This kind of prayer—petitionary prayer—isn't just about repeating the same request over and over. It's about coming before God with the kind of humble determination that says, "I trust you. I'm not letting go until I see you move."

Maybe as you're reading this, you can think of something—or someone—you've been praying for over and over again. And it's starting to feel like maybe God isn't listening. If that's you, hear

Jesus whispering through this story: "Don't quit. Keep knocking. Your Father hears you."

Because, as we're about to see, God loves giving good gifts to his kids. Jesus shows us this when he shifts gears again, back to the "good Father" image: "Which of you fathers, if your son asks for a fish, will give him a snake instead? Or if he asks for an egg, will give him a scorpion?" (Luke 11:11–12).

Now, my guess is that this would have been hilarious to the original audience. Jesus is cracking a joke here. In that culture, humor was rooted in irony and exaggerated contrast.[10] So when people heard this, they would've laughed out loud. It's kind of like saying, "Which of you parents would hand your toddler a Red Bull before bedtime?" It's absurd—and that's the point.

Jesus uses humor to make his audience lean in. He lightens the mood before landing something else deeply true: "If you then, though you are evil, know how to give good gifts to your children, how much more will your Father in heaven give the Holy Spirit to those who ask him!" (Luke 11:13). That phrase—"though you are evil"—is a bit jarring, right? But Jesus isn't calling us monsters. He's just being honest about human nature. We're flawed. We mess up. Even on our best parenting days, we fall short.

I think about moments when I've lost my patience with my kids. Times when money was tight and I was stressed and said things I wish I could take back. I wasn't at my best. I was trying to do right by my family, but in my own frustration, I failed. And yet even with all that imperfection, I still do my best to love and provide for them.

Jesus is saying, "If that's true for you—if you, in all your human messiness, still know how to give good gifts—then how much more will your perfect, loving Father in heaven give his best gifts to you?"[11] In this case, that best gift is the Holy Spirit. Jesus is using a classic rabbinic teaching technique called the "how much more" argument.[12] It's a way of saying that if something is true in a smaller, human way, then it's even truer in God's way. He's saying, "If even a tired, grouchy neighbor will eventually get up and help you, how much more will your Father in heaven, who loves you and who never gets tired, respond when you come to him?"

And that's the heartbeat of this whole passage. Jesus is showing us that prayer isn't some mechanical transaction where we say the right words and get the right results. Prayer is relational. It's the rhythm of sons and daughters coming to a loving Father. Friends coming to a faithful Friend and asking for help. Asking, seeking, knocking—not to twist God's arm but to stay close to his heart.

That's what Jesus is inviting us into. Prayer, for him, is all about relationship. Always has been. Always will be.

Now, my guess is that quite a few people reading this are thinking, "Okay, that's nice and all, but I'm still stuck on one thing. Why do I even need to ask God for stuff? Isn't he all-knowing? Doesn't he already know what I need before I open my mouth?"

That's a totally fair question. Because if God already knows everything, then what's the point of praying, right? Well, Jesus answers this question in an enlightening way through the story of a blind man named Bartimaeus in Mark 10. Here's the scene: Jesus is passing through Jericho with his disciples, and as usual, a massive crowd has gathered around him. Everyone wants a piece of his attention.

Meanwhile, sitting on the side of the road is this blind man, Bartimaeus. He's been begging for years, surviving off the generosity of others. When he hears that Jesus is coming, he yells at the top of his lungs, "Jesus, Son of David, have mercy on me!" (Mark 10:47). The crowd, of course, is not having it. They're trying to shut him up, telling him to quiet down, to stop making a scene. But Bartimaeus doesn't care. He just keeps going: "Son of David, have mercy on me!" (v. 48).

And then the story takes an amazing turn. Jesus hears the cry. He stops. Then he says something unexpected: "What do you want me to do for you?" (v. 51).

Now, if I'm in that crowd and I'm feeling a little bit skeptical about this so-called miracle worker, I'm thinking, "Really, Jesus? The guy's blind. He's literally blind. You can see that, right? You're the Son of God—surely you can connect the dots here."

And yet Jesus still asks: "What do you want me to do for you?"

Bartimaeus answers simply, "Rabbi, I want to see" (v. 51). Scripture says, "Immediately he received his sight and followed Jesus along the road" (v. 52).

Why does Jesus do that? Why does he ask a question when the answer seems so painfully obvious? Because Jesus isn't after the information—he's after the relationship. He doesn't make us ask because he's clueless about what we need. He makes us ask because he wants us to *invite him in*. To name the thing we long for. To open the tender, vulnerable part of our heart that says, "God, I need you here."

That's the essence of petitionary prayer. It's not about

convincing God to care—it's about participating in the relationship. When we ask, we're saying, "God, I trust you enough to be honest with you. I trust you enough to bring my need into the light." And that's what he wants. He wants conversation. He wants connection. He wants us to speak, not because he's unaware but because he loves hearing our voice.

So when Jesus says, "Give us today our daily bread," he's not just talking about literal food. He's teaching us how to live in daily dependence on our good Father.

John Frame summarizes it perfectly:

> Prayer is like a child going to his earthly father (cf. Matt. 6:9). The child wants something, and the father is eager to give. But the father does not give until the child asks. Anyone who is a father or mother understands the dynamic here. We want to give good things to our children, but even more we want a good relationship with them. Our heavenly Father wants the same. He does not want to be like a machine that dispenses goods, but he wants to really be our Father, a real person.[13]

It turns out that our Father *really* wants us to bring him our needs, our hopes, our fears, our longings—and to keep doing it. Because every time we ask, every time we seek, every time we knock, something happens in us. Our hearts soften. Our trust deepens. Our relationship with God grows stronger.

At the heart of "Give us today our daily bread" is a simple but radical invitation: to live one day at a time in honest dependence on a good Father. Jesus teaches us to pray not as isolated

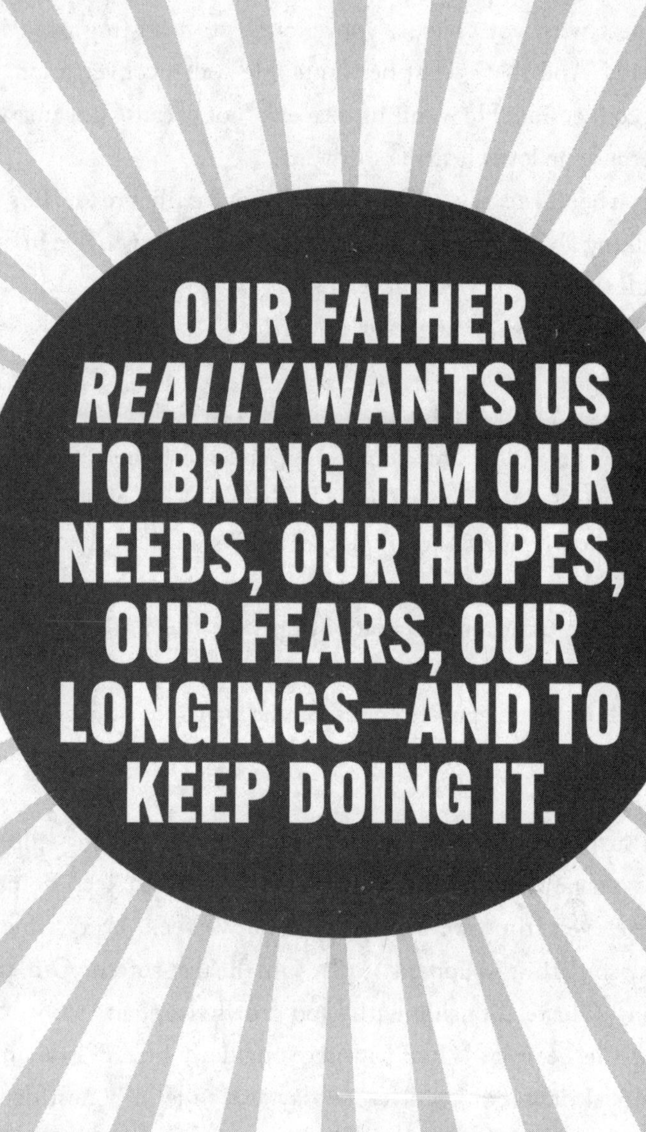
OUR FATHER
REALLY WANTS US
TO BRING HIM OUR
NEEDS, OUR HOPES,
OUR FEARS, OUR
LONGINGS—AND TO
KEEP DOING IT.

individuals but as a people, trusting God together for what we truly need, whether that's food, courage, forgiveness, patience, or grace for the next step. This prayer names our need without shame, invites persistence without manipulation, and grounds our asking in relationship rather than transaction. Daily bread isn't about stockpiling security for the future (Luke 12:16–21); it's about learning to trust that today's provision is enough because today's God is enough. Every time we ask, seek, and knock, we aren't informing God—we're opening ourselves to him. And in that daily rhythm of asking and receiving, our fear loosens its grip, our trust deepens, and we slowly learn to rest in the care of a Father who delights in giving good gifts to his children.

PRACTICAL PRAYER TIPS

Jesus told us to pray, "Give us today our daily bread," so let's do it. Begin by getting quiet. Take a few deep breaths. Place your hands open in your lap as a posture of trust and surrender.

Next, take a few minutes to ask God for something specific. Something real. Something that matters to you. This isn't about making a wish list or trying to twist God's arm. It's about opening your hands and heart before your Father and saying, "Here's what I need today."

Maybe it's something tangible, like provision or healing.

Maybe it's something deeper, like peace, forgiveness, direction, or the courage to keep going. Whatever it is, name it.

Take at least five minutes. And simply say again, "Father, this is what I need today."

Then trust that he hears you. Because he does. And trust that he's good. Because he is.

Now slowly and intentionally pray the full Lord's Prayer out loud:

> Our Father in heaven,
> hallowed be your name,
> your kingdom come,
> your will be done,
>   on earth as it is in heaven.
> *Give us today our daily bread.*
> And forgive us our debts,
>   as we also have forgiven our debtors.
> And lead us not into temptation,
>   but deliver us from the evil one.

Now linger on this phrase: "Give us today our daily bread."

Let it settle in. Ask yourself, "What do my community and I need from God today? Not this week. Not this year. Just today."

Maybe it's literal bread. Maybe it's peace. Or provision. Or clarity. Or strength. Or courage. Or help for someone you love.

Now turn that awareness into prayer:

> Father, today I bring you what I need, what I'm worried about, what I'm grateful for, and what I can't fix on my own. You know what I need before I ask—but still, I ask. Please provide what I need today, and teach me to trust you for tomorrow.

When you're done asking, take a deep breath and say, "Thank you for being the kind of Father who gives bread and not stones."

Let gratitude rise in your heart. Maybe even whisper a quiet "thank you" for everything that has already been provided today.

A TWO-WAY STREET CALLED FORGIVENESS

"Our Father in heaven,
hallowed be your name,
your kingdom come,
your will be done,
on earth as it is in heaven.
Give us today our daily bread.
And forgive us our debts,
as we also have forgiven our debtors."

—MATTHEW 6:9-12, EMPHASIS ADDED

Not forgiving is like drinking rat poison
and then waiting for the rat to die.

—ANNE LAMOTT

We're about to step into a weighty topic: forgiveness.

As we dig in, we'll see with great clarity that in the kingdom of God the appropriate response to being hurt is what we might call "regular and unlimited forgiveness." Oh boy.

When the topic of forgiveness comes up—let alone regular *and* unlimited forgiveness—most of us become a bit defensive. Here's why: Almost instantly, our minds race to the worst thing that has ever happened to us. We think, "Okay, I love the teachings of Christianity and all that. Obviously, Jesus was a brilliant ethicist and moral leader. But if God expects me to forgive *that* cruel person for *that* horrific act and then pretend it never happened and sit down to brunch together? Yeah, that's not going to happen. And honestly, I'm not sure I want to follow a God who seems so naive about what that would cost me physically, emotionally, and psychologically."

Friend, I get it. I've been there. But let me gently suggest that if that's where your head is, then chances are you don't really understand biblical forgiveness. Because biblical forgiveness, when rightly understood, isn't unsafe. It isn't enabling. It's actually good for you. It's the road to freedom.

Let's name a few things biblical forgiveness is not:[1]

- Biblical forgiveness doesn't mean you forget what happened. "Forgive and forget" is a cultural cliché, not a biblical command.
- Biblical forgiveness isn't denial. It's not pretending that sin isn't sin. Following Jesus doesn't mean pretending everything is okay when it's clearly not.

- Biblical forgiveness isn't condescending. It's not saying, "I forgive you," in a tone that really means, "See how big and generous I am, and how small you are."
- Biblical forgiveness isn't about abandoning justice. It still calls the wrongdoer to name the sin honestly—before God and before the one who was hurt—and to face whatever consequences God's law or human law requires.
- Biblical forgiveness doesn't always result in the relationship or trust being restored. Forgiveness and reconciliation are not the same thing. And I'm becoming increasingly convinced that blurring those lines is part of what keeps many Christians from practicing real and regular forgiveness.

That last point is crucially important, so I'm going to say it again. Even when forgiveness is offered, it's not always wise, safe, or possible to restore the relationship.

Dr. Darren Whitehead, founding pastor of Church of the City, says it like this:

- Forgiveness is personal. Reconciliation is mutual.
- Forgiveness is given. Reconciliation is earned.
- Forgiveness is always possible. Reconciliation is not always possible.
- Forgiveness is possible without reconciliation.
- Reconciliation is not possible without forgiveness.[2]

With those caveats in mind, what exactly is biblical forgiveness? The Greek word Paul uses for forgiveness—*charizomai*—has several definitions, including "to pardon, to show one's self

EVEN WHEN
FORGIVENESS IS
OFFERED, IT'S NOT
ALWAYS WISE,
SAFE, OR POSSIBLE
TO RESTORE THE
RELATIONSHIP.

gracious, to grant forgiveness."[3] It means to release someone from a moral or relational debt as an act of grace.

Simple, right?

Ha! Not at all.

But possible? Absolutely.

One thing I'm learning: The older I get, the more my happiness—and my mental health—depend on my ability to forgive. Young people, let me give you a heads-up: Eventually, life will land some punches. And as a follower of Jesus, you have to decide how to respond in a way that honors him. Because here's the truth: Jesus, Paul, and the other New Testament authors all assume that Christians will need to forgive regularly and generously. Paul puts it this way in Colossians 3:13: "Forgive one another if any of you has a grievance against someone. Forgive as the Lord forgave you." What I love about Paul is that he's no utopian dreamer. He doesn't say, "Hey, just invite Jesus into your heart and life will be a breeze, bruh!" No. He knows Christians still sin. We hurt each other. We get hurt. And because of that, we must forgive. But it's hard. We all know people who, in our view, don't deserve forgiveness.

So what do we do about them? The disciples had the same question. So Jesus gave them a master class on forgiveness, and thankfully Matthew was there taking notes.

As I mentioned earlier, when Jesus had to make an important point, he would often tell a funny story or parable. What follows is one of the funny ones. In my imagination, the original audience would have been rolling on the ground laughing at this comedy of satire and extremes—until it turns tragic at the end.

Let's look at Matthew 18:21–22: "Peter came to Jesus and asked, 'Lord, how many times shall I forgive my brother or sister who sins against me? Up to seven times?' Jesus answered, 'I tell you, not seven times, but seventy-seven times.'"

This was remarkable because in the first century, most rabbis taught that forgiveness had a three-strike limit. They based this on a few verses in the book of Amos, where God is seen forgiving Israel's enemies three times but then judgment follows.[4] Peter likely knew this. But by now, he's been around Jesus long enough to know there's always a twist. So he tries to impress the teacher: "Shall I forgive . . . up to seven times?" he asks.

Jesus responds, "Not seven . . . but seventy-seven times."

Let's be clear—this is hyperbole. He's not saying, "Track it in a spreadsheet, and at sin number seventy-eight, you're released from your Christian duty." Which means that—pro tip—Jesus is not advocating that you say to the love of your life, "Honey, you know I love you, but that was the seventy-eighth time you packed the dishwasher wrong. June was a rough month. Here's the chart. Do better. I'm going to hold a Jesus-approved grudge now!"

Rather, Jesus is saying, "Lose count. Forgive without limits."

Holding a grudge is one of the few investments that reliably depreciates while also costing us interest, yet sometimes we cling to grudges like rare coins.

Now, maybe you're thinking, "Jesus, with all due respect, that's naive. If you lived my life, you'd know that what you're asking isn't just unrealistic but dangerous for my emotional health."

And Jesus, seemingly anticipating that reaction, tells a story:

> The kingdom of heaven is like a king who wanted to settle accounts with his servants. As he began the settlement, a man who owed him ten thousand bags of gold was brought to him.

> Since he was not able to pay, the master ordered that he and his wife and his children and all that he had be sold to repay the debt. (Matthew 18:23–25)

In that era, one bag of gold (your Bible might call this unit of measure a "talent") was equivalent to twenty years' wages for a day laborer. So how much was ten thousand bags of gold worth? Let's do the math for context. The federal minimum wage in the USA is $7.25 per hour, which equals about $15,080 per year.

Multiplied by twenty, that is about $301,600.

Multiplied by ten thousand, that is over $3 billion.

Three billion dollars! That's enough coin to buy an NBA franchise!

> At this the servant fell on his knees before him. "Be patient with me," he begged, "and I will pay back everything." The servant's master took pity on him, canceled the debt and let him go. (vv. 26–27)

Jesus says the master forgave it. All of it. All three billion of it! That's some good news right there! But then here comes the dark twist.

> But when that servant went out, he found one of his fellow servants who owed him a hundred silver coins. He grabbed him and began to choke him. "Pay back what you owe me!" he demanded.
>
> His fellow servant fell to his knees and begged him, "Be patient with me, and I will pay it back."

> But he refused. Instead, he went off and had the man thrown into prison until he could pay the debt. When the other servants saw what had happened, they were outraged and went and told their master everything that had happened.
>
> Then the master called the servant in. "You wicked servant," he said, "I canceled all that debt of yours because you begged me to. Shouldn't you have had mercy on your fellow servant just as I had on you?" In anger his master handed him over to the jailers to be tortured, until he should pay back all he owed. (vv. 28–34)

This same guy—the *forgiven-three-billion-dollars* guy—walks outside and finds a coworker who owes him one hundred silver coins—about $6,000. This is a significant debt, yes, but with a little bit of planning, paying it off would be totally manageable.

The second servant pleads with him: "Be patient with me, and I will pay it back." It's word for word what the first guy just said to the master. But instead of extending mercy, he grabs the second servant, chokes him, and has him thrown in jail.

And when the master hears about it, he's furious: "Are you kidding me? After I forgave that massive debt, you couldn't let this guy off the hook for six grand?" So the king has him thrown into prison for the rest of his life.

And then Jesus says, "This is how my heavenly Father will treat each of you unless you forgive your brother or sister from your heart" (v. 35).

From your heart. In other words, forgiveness isn't just about releasing someone from a debt; it's about releasing yourself from the grip of anger.

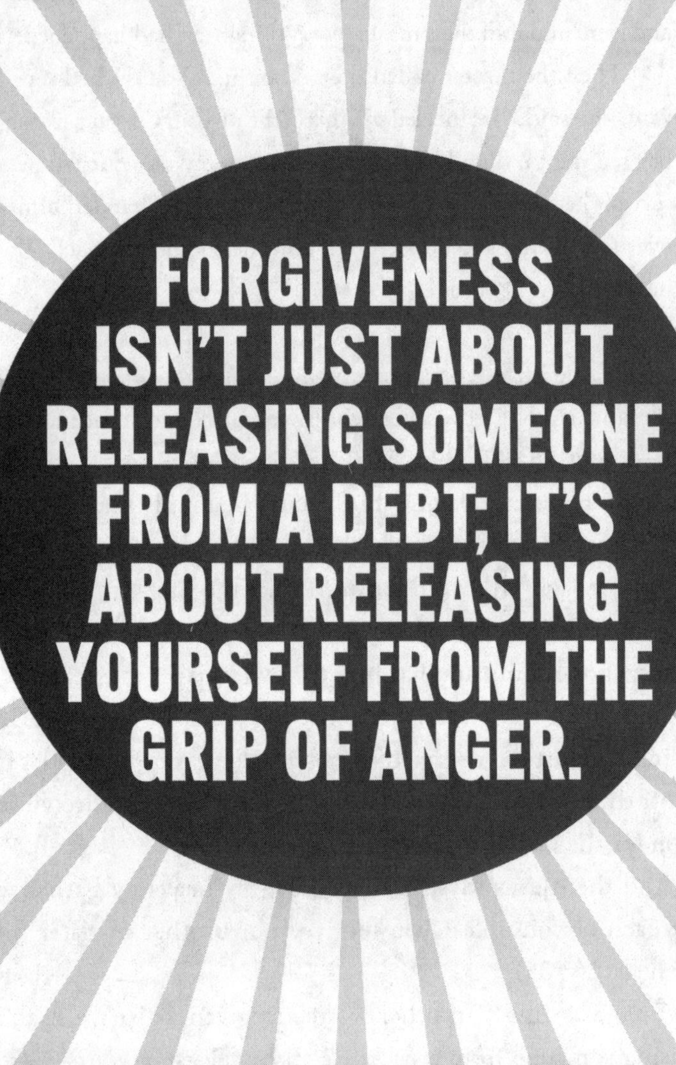
FORGIVENESS
ISN'T JUST ABOUT
RELEASING SOMEONE
FROM A DEBT; IT'S
ABOUT RELEASING
YOURSELF FROM THE
GRIP OF ANGER.

We've all seen people who've done this—people who've been deeply wounded but somehow chose to transform the evil done to them and stop it in its tracks. These people prove that the old saying "Hurt people hurt people" doesn't have to be true. Why? We live in a different kingdom. It's a kingdom where, by the power of the Holy Spirit, the cycle of pain can end with you.

Forgiveness is what breaks the cycle. And not just by releasing the one who hurt you—that's only the beginning. The deeper work is transforming the pain and, with God's help, repurposing it into something redemptive.

Theologian Ronald Rolheiser puts it like this:

> [Jesus] takes away the tensions and sins of the community by absorbing them, carrying them, transforming them, and not giving them back in kind. . . . Jesus did this by functioning like a water purifier, a filter of sorts . . . he took in hatred, held it, transformed it, and gave back love; he took in bitterness, held it, transformed it, and gave back graciousness; he took in curses, held them, transformed them, and gave back blessings; and he took in murder, held it, transformed it, and gave back forgiveness. Jesus resisted the instinct to give back in kind, hatred for hatred, curses for curses, jealousy for jealousy, murder for murder. He held and transformed these things rather than simply retransmitting them.[5]

That's the Christian design for taking tension and resentment out of our lives.

With the Holy Spirit's help, Christians can do hard things. We can change. We can live differently. Just because your dad was a cheater doesn't mean you have to be one. Just because your mum had a temper doesn't mean you're destined to rage too. And while that might sound lofty, every so often you catch a glimpse of it in the real world—and it takes your breath away. One of the most powerful examples I've ever encountered came out of South Africa in the early 1990s.[6]

On a stormy Sunday night in 1993, during the final years of apartheid, four gunmen burst into St. James Church in Cape Town during a packed worship service. They opened fire and hurled grenades into the congregation. By the time the chaos subsided, eleven people were dead and nearly sixty more were wounded. Among those killed was Marita Ackermann, wife of Dawie and mother of their three children.

Later that night, after hours at the hospital and after doing the impossible task of telling his children their mother was gone, Dawie returned to the church. A television crew was waiting for him in the foyer. A reporter raised a microphone and asked what he wanted to say to the men who had killed his wife.

Still wearing the shock of the night on his face, Dawie acknowledged the horror of what had happened—what had been taken from him and from his children. And then he said something no one expected: "But in the name of Jesus Christ, I forgive you, and I want you to turn yourself in."[7]

Those words aired nationwide within hours.

They arrived at a moment of enormous volatility. Just three months earlier, the assassination of Chris Hani had nearly fractured the country beyond repair. South Africans were bracing for retaliation. Anger was expected. Demands for revenge were expected.

Instead, from a grieving father and a wounded church came a

call to forgiveness. Not as a way of dismissing the violence or pretending the wounds didn't matter but as a refusal to add another drop of hatred to a nation already drowning in it.

In the days that followed, the church received stacks of hate mail from people who misunderstood what Christians mean by forgiveness. So the leaders began explaining it the way Scripture does: Forgiveness is never a shortcut around justice. It doesn't minimize evil; it trusts that justice ultimately belongs to God.

"There has to be justice before there is forgiveness," one leader said. "Even God deals with us like that. Forgiveness isn't free—it cost Christ something."[8]

Dawie Ackermann wasn't ignoring the evil done to his family. He wasn't numbing his loss. He was doing exactly what Jesus invites his followers to do: absorbing the pain rather than returning it, refusing to let violence multiply through him, and instead offering back to the world something transformed by grace.

He broke the cycle. And by the Spirit's power, we can too.

We've talked a lot about the hard part of forgiveness. But there's tremendous beauty on the other side. And when we forgive, not because someone deserves it but because we've been forgiven first, we begin to heal.

Modern medicine is catching up to this ancient wisdom. Dr. Karen Swartz, a researcher at Johns Hopkins, says, "There is an enormous physical burden to being hurt and disappointed."[9] According to their research, forgiveness is incredibly good for your soul and your body. Holding on to resentment increases your risk of heart attack, anxiety, and depression. Forgiveness improves sleep, lowers blood pressure, strengthens your immune system, and reduces pain levels. Forgiveness is literally healing.

WHEN WE
FORGIVE, NOT
BECAUSE SOMEONE
DESERVES IT BUT
BECAUSE WE'VE BEEN
FORGIVEN FIRST, WE
BEGIN TO HEAL.

We need to forgive often so that the pain and hurt of life on planet earth isn't a defining, destructive force in our lives. Forgiveness is basically canceling the debt you had already decided to bring up every holiday for the rest of your life. And because some wounds are so deep and painful, forgiveness becomes a daily choice not to:

- bring up the wound to the person who hurt you,
- weaponize their failure,
- gossip about the situation to justify your bitterness, or
- rehearse the offense over and over in your mind.

As Holocaust survivor Corrie ten Boom said, "Forgiveness is not an emotion. . . . Forgiveness is an act of the will, and the will can function regardless of the temperature of the heart."[10]

So how do we do it?

In *Forgiving What You'll Never Forget*, clinical psychologist and spiritual leader Dr. David Stoop offers a compelling road map for navigating the deep pain caused by betrayal, abuse, loss, and other seemingly unforgivable wounds.[11] Drawing from decades of counseling experience and biblical wisdom, Stoop challenges the cultural assumption that forgiveness means forgetting or excusing harm. Instead, he presents forgiveness as a courageous, soul-healing act that frees the wounded from the grip of bitterness and sets them on a path toward peace. Stoop's central message is clear: Forgiveness isn't about minimizing the wrong. It's about refusing to let pain define your life. This is one of the reasons I think Jesus built forgiveness into his regular prayer rhythm: because he knew we need it to ease our pain.

I get that "regular forgiveness" sounds intense. I certainly used to find forgiveness incredibly difficult. But since I've been praying the Lord's Prayer several times a day, it has become—dare I say it—really quite easy. Forgiveness becomes much simpler when you commit to it as a lifestyle; it's a muscle you can build. When we pray, "Forgive us our sins, as we forgive those who sin against us," we're stepping into a moment of transformation. We're choosing not to drink the poison of bitterness. We're participating in God's healing work. And it starts with our own hearts.

The surprise outcome of a life of regular and unlimited forgiveness is that we become lighter, more joyful people. To that end, I hope you will start a daily rhythm of forgiveness by using the Lord's Prayer as your vehicle.

PRACTICAL PRAYER TIPS

Take a breath. Relax your shoulders. Let go of your defenses.

Now slowly pray the Lord's Prayer aloud:

> Our Father in heaven,
> hallowed be your name,
> your kingdom come,
> your will be done,
> on earth as it is in heaven.
> Give us today our daily bread.
> *And forgive us our debts,*
> *as we also have forgiven our debtors.*

And lead us not into temptation,
but deliver us from the evil one.

Come back to this line: "And forgive us our debts, as we also have forgiven our debtors."

Sit with it. Let it soften you.

Ask, "God, is there anything I need to confess today?"

Let that question work in you for a few minutes.

Then try out this prayer:

> Father, I know I fall short. I miss the mark. I hurt others—sometimes on purpose, sometimes by accident. I ask for your forgiveness, not just to get off the hook but to be made whole. Clean me from the inside out. Let grace do its work. And now help me forgive the one who has hurt me. Not because they deserve it but because you first forgave me.

Pause.

Name the person, quietly or out loud.

Release them.

If it helps, picture yourself placing their offense into Jesus's hands.

Then say,

> I choose to forgive.
> Again today.
> Again tomorrow, if I need to.

Set them free from what they owe me, Lord—and in doing so, set me free too.

Now sit.
Breathe.
Let God's kindness cover the raw places until you feel free.

NINE

TEMPTATION

"Our Father in heaven,
hallowed be your name,
your kingdom come,
your will be done,
on earth as it is in heaven.
Give us today our daily bread.
And forgive us our debts,
as we also have forgiven our debtors.
And lead us not into temptation,
but deliver us from the evil one."

—MATTHEW 6:9-13, EMPHASIS ADDED

I can resist anything
except temptation.

—OSCAR WILDE

After teaching us to pray, "Forgive us our debts, as we also have forgiven our debtors," Jesus adds this curious line: "Lead us not into temptation."

It's a strange turn of phrase, isn't it? Is Jesus suggesting that God might lead us into temptation? Does God test us by dangling bad things in front of us to see if we will sin? That doesn't exactly sound like something a good Father would do.

Which brings me to something regrettable that happened to me—on a crisp fall day in East Nashville.

I've already told you about our little rescue dog, Rosie. She's half beagle, half something small-to-medium and unidentifiable, with the heart of a golden retriever crammed into her busy little body.

When we first got her, we installed one of those invisible fences—the kind with a buried wire and a collar that gives a mild zap if the animal crosses the boundary. It worked beautifully. Rosie was smart and learned her limits quickly. She'd bolt right up to the edge of the yard, nose twitching, stumpy tail wagging, and then stop just short of the property line. You could practically see the moral struggle in her eyes when a squirrel taunted her from the other side.

Eventually the transmitter on her collar died, but I never bothered replacing it because she simply never tried to leave our yard anymore. That worked great for two years. Then one day I received a text from Rosie's new friend Miss Maria, who lives a few doors down. When I arrived at Maria and Hector's to collect Rosie and bring her home, she looked extremely pleased with herself because she had realized she was free to roam the neighborhood without fear of an electric shock.

So we called the company that installed it all. Once they replaced the transmitter, we had to test Rosie to see if she remembered how it worked. The only way to do that was to tempt Rosie across the property line with her favorite toothbrush treats. It must have been a confusing moment for her. She trusted me, and there I was, coaxing her toward a jolt. As she approached the fence, her collar beeped and she started shaking. I had led her into temptation—the great sin of leaving our front yard—and as her adoptive father, I didn't feel good about it.

So here's a question that has stumped me for years. Why on earth does Jesus have us pray that our heavenly Father won't do stuff like that to us? Here's what I've learned about this peculiar phrase over the last twelve months. When Jesus teaches us to pray this line, the Greek word used for "temptation" is *peirasmos*. This word has a broad range of meaning, and depending on the context it can mean either "temptation" or "testing."

Most scholars agree that *testing* fits best here.[1] God doesn't tempt anyone to sin. Jesus's little brother James made that clear when he wrote, "When tempted, no one should say, 'God is tempting me.' For God cannot be tempted by evil, nor does he tempt anyone" (James 1:13). Our Father is not in the business of tempting us. But he does allow his people to be tested. James speaks to this as well: "Consider it pure joy, my brothers and sisters, whenever you face trials of many kinds, because you know that the testing of your faith produces perseverance. Let perseverance finish its work so that you may be mature and complete, not lacking anything" (James 1:2–4).

There's a difference between temptation and testing. Both involve pressure, but the purpose is different: One is destructive, the other redemptive.

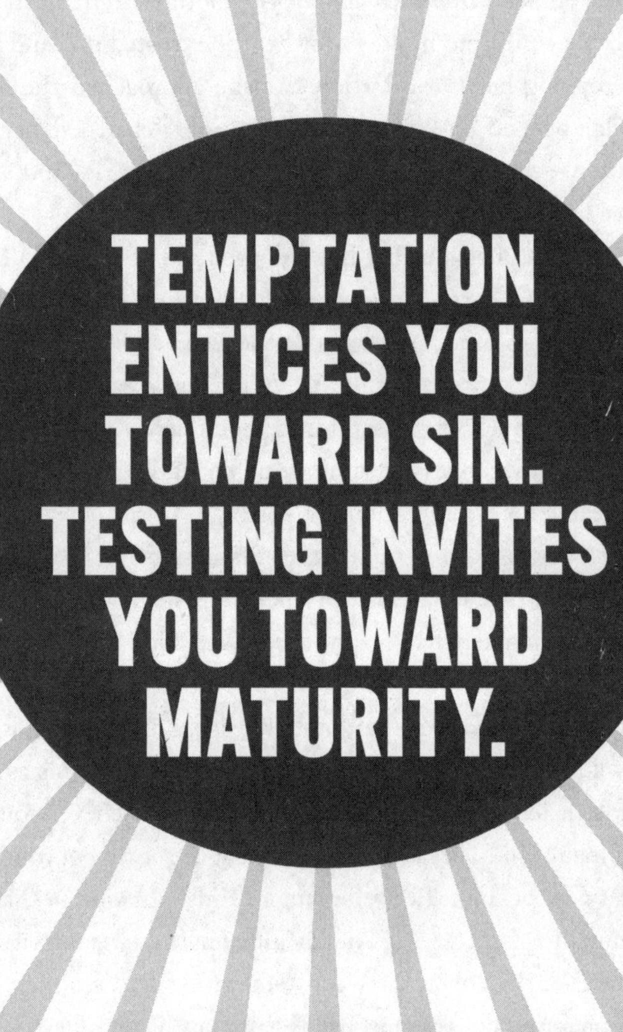
TEMPTATION
ENTICES YOU
TOWARD SIN.
TESTING INVITES
YOU TOWARD
MATURITY.

Temptation is designed to pull you down.
Testing is designed to grow you up.
Temptation entices you toward sin.
Testing invites you toward maturity.

So when Jesus prays, "Lead us not into temptation," he's not saying, "Lord, never let anything hard happen to me." He's saying, "Father, don't let me face a test so severe that it breaks me. Protect me from the kind of trial that will destroy me." This is a prayer for protection from the dark forces of evil. It's not a prayer to rid our lives of difficulty. Theologian and author N. T. Wright put it this way: "Jesus intends his followers to recognize not only the reality of evil but the reality of his victory over it."[2]

This part of the Lord's Prayer is a humble recognition of spiritual vulnerability, that apart from God's guidance and strength, our hearts are easily pulled off course. In other words, it's like praying, "Father, don't let me go where I can't handle the pressure." Or "Please keep me out of situations that I lack the moral strength to withstand." This isn't a fear-based prayer. It's wisdom. It's the prayer of someone who knows their limits and trusts God's leadership more than their own resilience.

So if God doesn't tempt us, why do we still feel pulled toward things that aren't good for us? Because temptation rarely feels like an outright rebellion at first; it's more often a minor rewording of the rules so we can technically still be on God's side while doing what we want. Let's talk about where that tendency comes from—and what God wants to do about it. Scripture tells us that without the restoring work of the Holy Spirit, we are basically led by our desires and emotions (Galatians 5:16–17). We're driven by what we want and how we feel. That's why the Bible insists we need to be made new, given a new heart—a theological idea known as regeneration.

Jesus didn't die just to take away our sin; he came to regenerate us, to transform us from the inside out by the Holy Spirit. Regeneration is about God taking a heart of stone and replacing it with a heart that's soft and responsive to him. When your heart is renewed, your desires change. You start wanting things that are good and holy, and your appetite for the broken-but-delicious stuff that used to tempt you begins to fade. Timothy Keller spoke to this: "What you need to drive out an old passion is a new passion—a greater passion. What you need is an over-mastering positive passion."[3]

As our hearts are regenerated, those old temptations lose their grip, and healthier, holier passions take their place. And life gets a whole lot simpler and healthier as sin loses its power.

Now, talking about sin isn't exactly fashionable in our cultural moment. But maybe this definition that is widely attributed to Ignatius of Loyola will help: "Sin is unwillingness to trust that what God wants for me is only my deepest happiness."[4] Exactly. The most damaging thing sin does isn't that it breaks a rule; it's that it keeps us from joy, peace, and wholeness. God doesn't hate sin because it breaks a commandment. He hates sin because it breaks us. Sin pulls us out of alignment with how the world was designed to work.

When we learn to master those knee-jerk impulses that threaten to ruin our relationships and our peace—when we walk in step with the Spirit—it's like getting a foretaste of heaven. It's a step toward restoration. Toward becoming whole again. As we

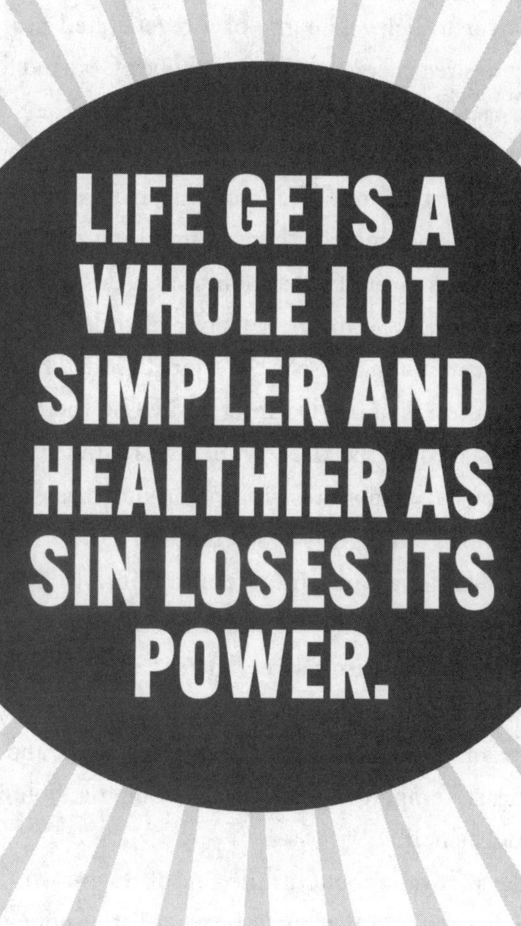
LIFE GETS A WHOLE LOT SIMPLER AND HEALTHIER AS SIN LOSES ITS POWER.

deal with sin and pursue holiness, we become freer and more available to do good with our lives.

Note that regeneration is the opposite of religion. The religious view of God says he's far away, handing out random rules, keeping score, and waiting for you to mess up. Regeneration is about a God who comes near to help. The gift of a regenerated heart is this: Your deepest desire becomes the desire to obey God and follow the pattern of Jesus. That's what transformation looks like.

As John Mark Comer says, "Our strongest desires are not actually our deepest desires."[5] Yes, you may have strong desires in the moment, but underneath, there's something deeper. A longing for self-control. A hunger for holiness. A desire for your love to be rightly ordered. Scripture calls our disordered desires "the flesh"—the part of us that resists the way of God. The journey of spiritual formation is about learning to live by the Spirit rather than being enslaved by the flesh. When we're under Jesus's leadership, emotions and appetites stop being our masters and start becoming servants of a rightly ordered heart.

Praying, "Lead us not into temptation," isn't just about avoiding bad stuff. It's about leaning into God's strength to live differently. Temptation isn't some ancient idea relegated to the wilderness stories in the Bible. It's with us. It's in our phones, our thoughts, our Netflix queues, our conversations, and yes, even our tax returns. Temptation isn't always dramatic. Sometimes it's embarrassingly small.

Most days, I walk about a mile out of downtown Nashville to grab lunch—for two reasons: to save a little money (because downtown Nashville lunch prices are crazy) and to clear my head. A few weeks ago, I ordered a salad with chicken—eight dollars. I asked for extra chicken—two more dollars. When the bill came, I was charged only eight. I knew I should speak up, but I didn't. In my head I reasoned, "Maybe they misheard the accent. Maybe I didn't say 'extra chicken' clearly enough. Maybe they didn't give me extra chicken." So I kept quiet and walked away, congratulating myself on getting a deal.

But that night, as I prayed this part of the Lord's Prayer and thought about the little compromises of my day, the Holy Spirit brought it back to mind. That cheap salad suddenly felt a whole lot more expensive. The next day, I walked back to the restaurant and paid the extra two dollars. The cashier looked at me like I had lost my mind. But it was worth it.

"And lead us not into temptation" is such a gift in the Lord's Prayer. It acknowledges what we're often too proud to admit: We are not as strong as we think we are. It makes peace with our limits. It recognizes that we have blind spots. And it invites God to meet us there. It says, "Father, please don't let me walk into something I can't handle."

I don't need help spotting the big temptations—I usually see those coming. The small ones are what sneak up on me. The subtle ones. The ones that sound like my own voice and wear the disguise of common sense. The ones that feel harmless but slowly bend my character a centimeter at a time. Those are the places where my blind spots mostly live. And those are the places where I need God's help most.

Self-evaluation is hard. That's why we need God's help. One of the Holy Spirit's key roles is to help us see our sin so we can deal with it. The point isn't to shame us but to set us free. Jesus said about the Spirit, "When he comes, he will convict the world concerning sin and righteousness and judgment" (John 16:8 ESV). Conviction isn't condemnation. It's clarity. It's the Spirit's gentle whisper: "You're drifting. Come back." That's why when we pray, "Lead us not into temptation," we're also saying, "Search me. Show me what I can't see. Make me whole." Now when I pray this part of the Lord's Prayer, I ask the Holy Spirit to reveal my blind spots, because I want to see so that I can be free.

This line of the Lord's Prayer—"Lead us not into temptation"—has become one of the most honest prayers I pray. It's me admitting the truth about myself: I am not as strong, insightful, or self-aware as I wish I were. There are places I shouldn't go, decisions I shouldn't make alone, pressures that could undo me. Admitting this truth about myself is one way I meet God's kindness amid my brokenness. Because this is not the prayer of a terrified child begging for rescue. It's the prayer of a beloved child trusting a good Father: "Walk with me. Guide me. Keep me close. Lead me where you know I can flourish."

PRACTICAL PRAYER TIPS

With all of this in mind, take a moment to practice praying about temptation and sin.

Start by getting still. Take a few deep breaths. Place both feet flat on the floor. Open your hands. Ask God to meet you right where you are.

Now pray the full Lord's Prayer slowly, out loud:

Our Father in heaven,
hallowed be your name,
your kingdom come,
your will be done,
  on earth as it is in heaven.
Give us today our daily bread.
And forgive us our debts,
  as we also have forgiven our debtors.
And lead us not into temptation,
  but deliver us from the evil one.

Now focus on this phrase: "And lead us not into temptation."

Let it echo in your soul. It's a reminder that we are not invincible. That there are moments, relationships, habits, and thoughts we can't walk through alone.

Start here:

Father, I acknowledge my weakness. I know I'm not immune to temptation. I invite you to guide my steps away from anything that might pull me from your path. And if I do stumble, meet me there. Strengthen me. Rescue me. Walk with me.

Now ask, "Where am I most vulnerable right now? What habits, relationships, or patterns tend to trip me up?"

Speak honestly with God. He already knows. You're just bringing it into the light.

Pray this:

Holy Spirit, open my eyes. Show me what I can't see. Reveal my blind spots. Search me. Convict me. And lead me not into temptation but into freedom.

You might also want to pray Psalm 139:23–24:

> Search me, God, and know my heart;
> test me and know my anxious thoughts.
> See if there is any offensive way in me,
> and lead me in the way everlasting.

Now pause. Breathe. Let God speak. And let the restorative work of baring yourself to the light begin.

TEN

OUR SKIRMISH WITH EVIL

"Our Father in heaven,
hallowed be your name,
your kingdom come,
your will be done,
on earth as it is in heaven.
Give us today our daily bread.
And forgive us our debts,
as we also have forgiven our debtors.
And lead us not into temptation,
but deliver us from the evil one."

—MATTHEW 6:9-13, EMPHASIS ADDED

Enemy-occupied territory—
that is what this world is.

—C. S. LEWIS

And now we come to the final phrase of the Lord's Prayer: "Deliver us from the evil one." That means we will now be chatting about a concept that is often referred to as "spiritual warfare."

My understanding of spiritual warfare didn't start from a place of certainty; it started from confusion. "Evil forces" in my childhood imagination were filed away somewhere in the same creative corner of my brain as Santa and Gargamel from *The Smurfs*—both colorful characters who made for entertaining stories but didn't have much to do with real life.

When I was a kid, evil was mostly a category for fairy tales and the PG-13 movies I wasn't allowed to watch. The devil felt like a cartoonish villain with a pitchfork—more of a Halloween costume than a real presence to take seriously. And in our home—we were good, solid Methodists who valued faith, manners, and being on time—talk of demons wasn't exactly part of the nightly rhythm between mouthfuls of quiche.

But as I grew older, life started handing me experiences I didn't have language for.

There were seasons when I felt opposed in a way that didn't match the circumstances. Days when everything on the outside looked ordinary, yet a heaviness—discouragement, confusion, anxiety—would press in out of nowhere like someone had slipped a weighted blanket over my soul. It wasn't dramatic. It wasn't cinematic. It was subtle, quiet, even seemingly reasonable . . . and yet unmistakably real.

Sometimes I watched people I loved unravel under pressures that felt strangely targeted, as though something was intentionally coming after their joy or peace or identity. And sometimes, if I slowed down long enough to pay attention, I could sense that the struggle in my own life wasn't just internal; something was pushing back. There were days when simply staying upright in hope or peace felt like an act of resistance. Like the real miracle wasn't charging forward in victory; it was finding the strength to stand when everything in me wanted to collapse.

Maybe you've felt that too. The resistance that shows up when you try to change. The discouragement that arrives the moment hope begins to rise. The tug-of-war between who you are and who you were meant to be.

There's a moment in every Christian's life when we realize this: Either Scripture is right about evil, or the world makes absolutely no sense. And God, in his kindness, often prepares us to see that truth long before we understand what's happening.

In my case, he started leaving clues in the oddest places—starting, apparently, with my birth certificate. When I was growing up, my mum—Glenys Smallbone, who has always delighted in a good detail—loved pointing out that I was born on July 7, 1977: 7/7/77—a birthdate that, depending on who heard it, either mildly impressed others or seemed spiritually significant.

That might explain why, as a teenager, I occasionally drew special attention from the more enthusiastic members of our church's intercessory prayer team. Wonderful people. Faithful people. Slightly intense people. One gentleman, who I'm fairly certain kept a running spreadsheet of end-times prophecies, once pulled me aside after church and said, with total sincerity, "Mate, with a birthdate like yours, God has marked you for a significant end-times assignment." Then he leaned in and added, "I think you may be called to battle the Antichrist at Armageddon."

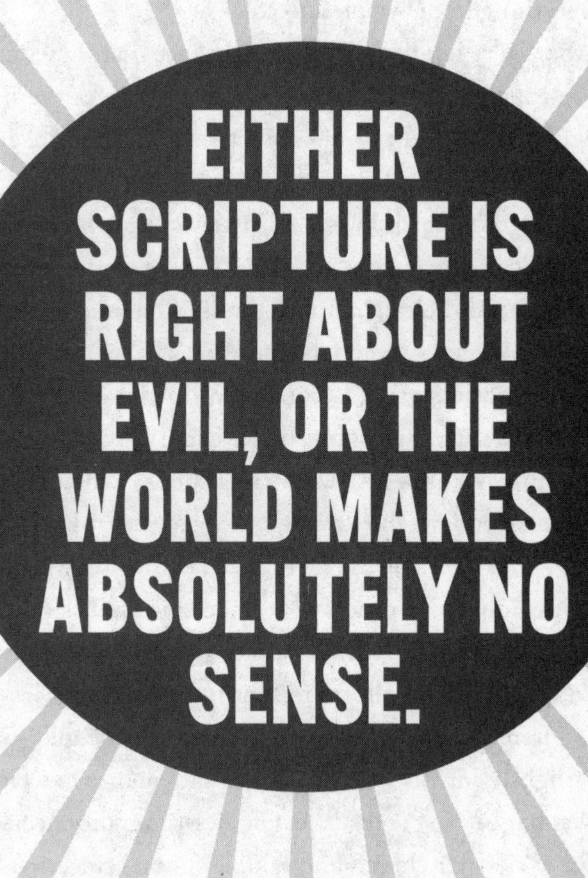
EITHER
SCRIPTURE IS
RIGHT ABOUT
EVIL, OR THE
WORLD MAKES
ABSOLUTELY NO
SENSE.

I was fifteen. My only spiritual weapon at the time was a WWJD bracelet. I wasn't sure whether to feel chosen or to sprint out of there. Even though his comment was wildly over the top, it was my first glimpse that there might be more going on in the world than what I could see. Maybe the spiritual realm wasn't a side plot of Christian faith; maybe it was part of the actual story. Maybe life wasn't just difficult; maybe it was contested.

Pastor Timothy Keller, a deeply intellectual and pragmatic man, noted that "modern people are uncomfortable with the existence of evil, let alone the existence of the Devil. Yet, the Bible teaches that we cannot fully understand the world we live in unless we realize that there are supernatural agents of evil."[1] Jesus obviously thought it should be talked about. So even though we may not like addressing it, we need to. Because the world we occupy is tricky to understand if we don't acknowledge that there is evil at work.

While many of us don't like thinking about the devil and his schemes, deep down we have to admit that we've endured seasons when it felt like we were in the middle of a war against unseen powers of evil—like there was something or someone out there trying to take us down. It's a tension we live in as Christians navigating a dark world. The Bible certainly backs this up, even offering a warning: "Be alert and of sober mind. Your enemy the devil prowls around like a roaring lion looking for someone to devour" (1 Peter 5:8).

My guess is that the folks reading this chapter are divided into several distinct groups on this issue of spiritual warfare. Some are hesitant, some are cautious, and still others are all in—ready to storm the gates of hell as soon as you receive your marching orders. This is nothing new, by the way. Spiritual warfare has always been a topic that has divided religious gatherings. It did even in Jesus's day!

When Jesus taught his disciples to pray, "Deliver us from the evil one," his Jewish audience would have heard that line through the lens of one of three spiritual worldviews, depending on their branch of Judaism.[2] Even more, each group probably disagreed with Jesus on what evil actually was and how it was supposed to be dealt with.

Pete Greig notes that on one side were the Sadducees. These were the upper-class elites, part of the priestly class. They held power in the temple, aligned themselves with Roman authorities, and were known for playing the political game to preserve their influence. They were also the skeptics of their time. Sophisticated. Intellectual. They didn't believe in angels, demons, or the afterlife. They figured all that "spiritual warfare" talk was primitive—superstitious leftovers from less enlightened minds. So when Jesus said, "Deliver us from the evil one," I imagine they rolled their eyes and thought, "This guy still believes in the devil? How adorable! Evil isn't cosmic—it's just bad politics and weak leadership. What we need is better governance, not weird supernatural prayers."

At the other extreme were the Essenes. They were the spiritual radicals—think first-century mystics living out in the wilderness. While the Sadducees downplayed spiritual forces, the Essenes saw everything as a cosmic showdown between good and evil. If it were up to them, the Lord's Prayer would be trimmed down to just one line: "Yahweh, deliver us from the evil one. Amen." That was the only thing that really mattered to them.

And right in the middle were the Pharisees. They believed in the supernatural: angels, demons, heaven, hell. But their approach to evil was about protection through personal holiness. They believed that if you followed the law—613 commandments, to be exact—you could evil-proof your life. So most likely the Pharisees were fine with praying, "Deliver us from the evil one," because, for them, that meant "Help me stick to the rules." It wasn't a cry for rescue. It was more like, "God, give me the strength to live by the checklist."

Most of us fall into one of those three camps. Some of us think like Sadducees. We're comfortable with a loving, wise God, but we prefer talking psychology, sociology, or policy reform. Evil as a spiritual force is a little over the top. Others of us lean Essene. We'd rather pray about a crisis than sign a petition and attend a rally. The real battle, for us, is in the heavenlies. And then there are the Pharisee types, those of us who acknowledge the spiritual realm but whose response is to double down on personal discipline: reading the Bible, making moral choices, keeping our lives "clean." The idea is, if we can just behave well enough, maybe the Evil One will leave us alone most of the time.

But here's what fascinates me: Jesus teaches prayer in a space where all three worldviews are swirling—and he challenges every one of them. He doesn't say that evil is only political, or only spiritual, or only avoided through moral performance. He simply says to ask the Father to deliver us from it. Because the real solution to evil isn't our sophistication, our mysticism, or our rule-following. It's the blood of Jesus.

Jesus is saying, "When you come up against evil—and you will—you don't have to intellectualize it, escape from it, or try to

THE REAL SOLUTION TO EVIL ISN'T OUR SOPHISTICATION, OUR MYSTICISM, OR OUR RULE-FOLLOWING. IT'S THE BLOOD OF JESUS.

earn your way through it. You pray, and you ask your Father to deliver you. Because he can. And he will."

I've always appreciated the way C. S. Lewis talks about spiritual warfare. In his preface to *The Screwtape Letters*, he points out, "There are two equal and opposite errors into which our race can fall about the devils. One is to disbelieve in their existence. The other is to believe, and to feel an excessive and unhealthy interest in them."[3]

Option A, he argues, is to ignore the forces of evil—to pretend they don't exist—and to use cartoon images of a "devil" with horns and hooves as an apologetic about how only stupid people could believe in this stuff.

Option B is to take an unhealthy interest in everything demonic, which—as some of us know firsthand—can be just as unhelpful in the long run.

So which one is right? Neither one. Lewis argues for a third way. Essentially, it's this: A life modeled on Jesus and rooted in a biblical worldview should include a sober recognition of the reality of spiritual opposition without abandoning common sense.

I'm with him, because I have seen tremendous damage done by well-meaning Christians who accurately discerned that evil was at work but then operated without good judgment. Or to put it another way, *There is nothing quite as dangerous as a Christian who operates in the gifts of the Spirit in the absence of the fruit of the Spirit.* The apostle Paul pointed to this when he said, "If I speak in the tongues of men or of angels, but do not have love, I am only a resounding gong or a clanging cymbal" (1 Corinthians 13:1).

To be clear, the authors of Scripture are united in the understanding that we are in the midst of a spiritual battle with the Evil

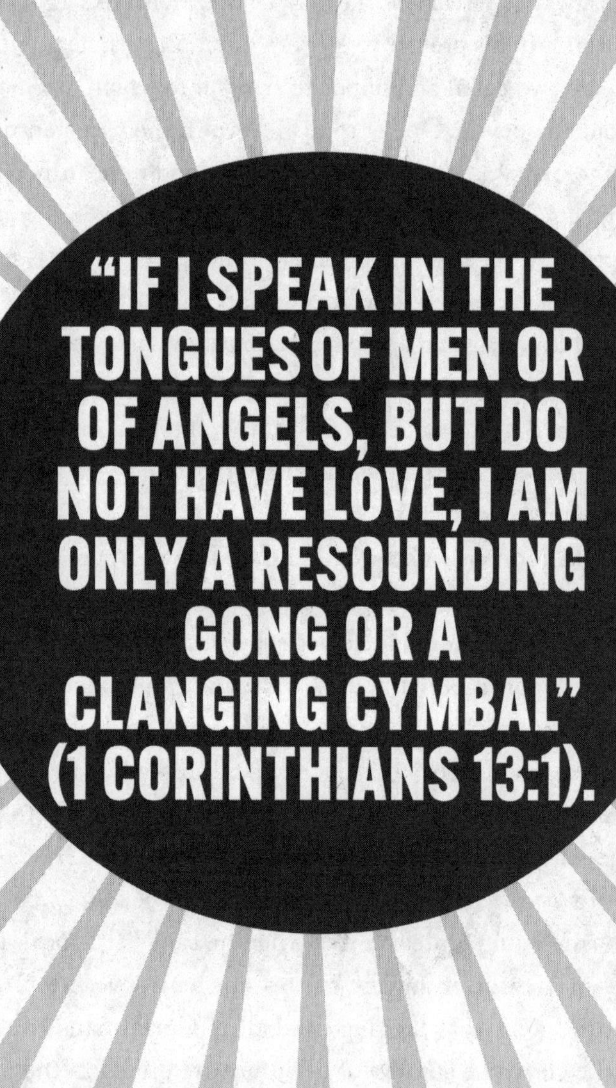
"IF I SPEAK IN THE
TONGUES OF MEN OR
OF ANGELS, BUT DO
NOT HAVE LOVE, I AM
ONLY A RESOUNDING
GONG OR A
CLANGING CYMBAL"
(1 CORINTHIANS 13:1).

One. Jesus himself launched his whole ministry with forty days of spiritual warfare in the wilderness. Matthew, Mark, and Luke all describe how after Jesus's baptism, the Spirit led him into the wilderness, where he fasted for forty days and nights. During that time, Satan came to him and tempted him in three significant ways. These temptations were designed to challenge Jesus's identity, his relationship with the Father, and his mission.

And those three things Jesus had to face are likely the same things being attacked in all of us right now:

Our identity: Who am I?

Our relationship with God: Does God really care about me?

Our purpose: What am I meant to do with my life?

All of us battle these thoughts, and Scripture names them as what they truly are: spiritual attacks. All the New Testament authors speak of the reality of evil forces. So let's unpack "deliver us from the evil one" by quickly studying Paul's classic passage on spiritual warfare in Ephesians 6. Let's start in verse 10: "Finally, be strong in the Lord and in his mighty power. Put on the full armor of God, so that you can take your stand against the devil's schemes" (vv. 10–11).

As we walk through this passage, I want you to notice the repetition of one word: *stand*. Paul doesn't say to charge, attack, or chase. He says "stand." Stand your ground. Stand firm. Spiritual warfare, in Paul's view, is largely about holding on to what God has already given us. It's a defensive posture: resisting, not retreating. Klyne Snodgrass notes that "to 'stand' connotes strength, stability, and success in a conflict or difficulty."[4]

Then Paul continues, "For our struggle is not against flesh and blood, but against the rulers, against the authorities, against the powers of this dark world and against the spiritual forces of evil in the heavenly realms" (v. 12).

Many of us are surprised there's even a struggle. Sure, we know faith can be tough—praying consistently, practicing forgiveness, fighting temptation—but we don't often realize that these struggles are part of something larger.

Paul is showing us that these "small" battles fit into a cosmic war: "Therefore put on the full armor of God, so that when the day of evil comes, you may be able to stand your ground, and after you have done everything, to stand" (v. 13). Armor, not weapons, is the emphasis here. Why? Because armor helps us stay standing when life gets intense.

Let's look at the gear. Truth is our first line of defense: "Stand firm then, with the belt of truth buckled around your waist" (v. 14a).

This means we have to constantly fill our minds with what's true: Jesus rose from the dead; we are loved and adopted by God; we are not defined by the lies or labels others put on us. Without truth—about who God is and who we are—we won't be able to stand.

Next: ". . . with the breastplate of righteousness in place . . ." (v. 14b).

The breastplate protects the heart. If we look at this through a spiritual lens, *righteousness* shields us from the Enemy's attacks, especially from accusations about our integrity or worth. Paul says to the Romans, "This righteousness is given through faith in Jesus Christ to all who believe" (Romans 3:22). We don't earn righteousness. It's gifted. We wear it like a covering, a spiritual armor that reminds us we're right with God through Jesus.

Next: ". . . and with your feet fitted with the readiness that comes from the gospel of peace" (v. 15).

This is about mobility—being ready to go where needed, bringing the gospel of peace. Readiness means we're eager and prepared to share the good news with others. Paul says that this willingness helps us stand under attack.

Next we read, "In addition to all this, take up the shield of faith, with which you can extinguish all the flaming arrows of the evil one" (v. 16).

Faith protects us from the "flaming arrows": doubt, temptation, discouragement, pride, tragedy. Whatever the Enemy throws, faith blocks and extinguishes it.

From there, we need to "take the helmet of salvation . . ." (v. 17a).

This is about identity. If you've trusted Jesus, your salvation is secure. That confidence protects your thoughts. It guards your mind against fear, anxiety, and condemnation. It reminds you: *I belong to God.*

And finally comes one weapon of offense: ". . . and the sword of the Spirit, which is the word of God" (v. 17b).

This is our weapon. Jesus modeled how to use it when he faced the devil in the wilderness. There, he quoted Scripture to confront every temptation Satan threw at him. When the Enemy attacks, we don't argue—we speak truth.

Paul adds one more vital piece of equipment: "And pray in the Spirit on all occasions with all kinds of prayers and requests. With this in mind, be alert and always keep on praying for all the Lord's people" (v. 18). Prayer is how we activate the armor. We pray, "Deliver us from the evil one." In this, we are recognizing the battle and putting on our armor. It's how we stay alert and connected. It's how we stand our ground.

PRACTICAL PRAYER TIPS

You know the drill! Let's pray the full Lord's Prayer slowly, out loud:

> Our Father in heaven,
> hallowed be your name,
> your kingdom come,
> your will be done,
>   on earth as it is in heaven.
> Give us today our daily bread.
> And forgive us our debts,
>   as we also have forgiven our debtors.
> And lead us not into temptation,
>   *but deliver us from the evil one.*

Now focus on the last phrase: "but deliver us from the evil one."

As we pray this line, we remember that we belong to the God who is greater than anything we'll face. So we don't pray out of fear. We pray from a place of confidence and trust.

When you pray, "Deliver me from the evil one," you're not just naming a fear—you're reaching for a lifeline. This isn't a prayer for spiritual superheroes. It's for the exhausted parent. The anxious student. The burned-out pastor. The person quietly asking, "Is something working against me right now?"

Here's how I often pray it:

> Father, deliver me from anything that's trying to pull me away from you. Keep me from the Enemy's lies, traps, and distractions. Guard my heart. Protect my mind. Lead me in truth. Walk with me through this day. Amen.

This is a battle, and you're not fighting alone. You are loved. You are equipped. So walk into your day with confidence, knowing that "the one who is in you is greater than the one who is in the world" (1 John 4:4).

ELEVEN

OVER TO YOU

Many persons believe in the efficacy of prayer, but not many pray.

—E. M. BOUNDS

Well, friend, you've made it.

We've walked line by line through the most famous prayer in the world. We've slowed down, marveled, reflected, repented, requested, wrestled with our choices, forgiven, engaged in spiritual warfare, and hopefully laughed a little along the way. And now, here we are at the final chapter. But this isn't really the end.

This is the handoff. From here on out, it's over to you. You get to join the great adventure of talking with your heavenly Father the way Jesus did. I hope you'll try it, because I can't think of anything more wasteful than knowing a ton of information about prayer but never praying. That would be like having a master's degree in dentistry but working at an ice cream shop.

My life changed when I prayed this prayer exclusively for one year. It moved me from an awkward pray-er to a man whose first instinct is to chat with God about whatever is occupying my thoughts and feelings. Here are some best practices I've learned along the way that I encourage you to remember as you start the thirty-day prayer guide following this chapter.

Pray the entire Lord's Prayer—in order—every time.

Here's an example of what that looks like for me. Let's imagine that a coworker has hurt my feelings in a meeting. Let's call him Jean-Raphael for the purposes of this example. I'll note whatever triggered me, and I'll talk to God in the following way the next chance I get to be alone. This entire process often takes me only a few minutes:

OUR FATHER IN HEAVEN

My Father, who is as close as the air I breathe, I'm just going to take a beat and acknowledge that you're right here with me. You were with me in that meeting just now. Thanks for being close. Thanks for caring about the small details of my life. Thanks for looking out for me. Thanks for being Jean-Raphael's Father too.

HALLOWED BE YOUR NAME

You are holy and I respect you greatly.

YOUR KINGDOM COME

Father, I'm asking that the way you designed the world to be—peaceful and harmonious—will be true of my working relationship with Jean-Raphael. But I've got to tell you, he really ticked me off in that meeting when he criticized my performance last week without talking about it with me first.

YOUR WILL BE DONE, ON EARTH AS IT IS IN HEAVEN

That being said, I know he has his reasons for doing what he did. But I am *so* angry and hurt by him right now. Honestly, I want to destroy that muppet in a group text. But I ask that your will, not mine, be done in this situation.

GIVE US TODAY OUR DAILY BREAD

Holy Spirit, help me offer him the most generous explanation for his behavior. Please show me the right next step in this conflict.

AND FORGIVE US OUR DEBTS, AS WE ALSO HAVE FORGIVEN OUR DEBTORS

Forgive me for calling Jean-Raphael a muppet. I forgive him the moral debt he owes me for hurting me. I pray that you'll bless him.

AND LEAD US NOT INTO TEMPTATION

Please help me figure out the best response to all of this. Help me not to make this worse.

(At this point I usually take a moment to think through my options for how I can respond. And because I have done the previous steps, I usually find that my heart is more generous than it was forty-five seconds earlier.)

BUT DELIVER US FROM THE EVIL ONE

Father, I ask that you protect me from the Evil One. Help me stand. Show me what is true in this situation. Guard my heart and protect my mind. Amen.

Of course, this prayer isn't limited to difficult coworkers or awkward meetings. That's just one doorway into it. I've prayed the Lord's Prayer while making big decisions, while lying awake with anxiety, while staring at bank statements, while trying to forgive myself, while grieving things that couldn't be fixed, and while simply trying to figure out what faithfulness looks like on an ordinary Tuesday. Wherever there is confusion, desire, fear, gratitude, temptation, or longing, this prayer has room for it. The Lord's Prayer is less like a special-occasion prayer and more like a daily operating system—something sturdy enough to hold the weight of your whole life, not just your worst moments. I encourage you to pray it several times a day.

Let it echo through your commute, your work, your interactions. I usually pray the Lord's Prayer as soon as I wake up, on my drive to work, whenever things trigger me throughout the day, and before I fall asleep.

In my first prayer, I usually pray about the day ahead.

In my last prayer, I usually pray about the day I just had.

Everything else is in response to whatever life brings my way. When life gets weird, I pray the Lord's Prayer.

Reach for it in conflict. When anger rises, use this prayer as a framework to navigate the moment.

Lean on it when faith feels thin. When God feels far, use this prayer to reconnect with your Father, who is as close as the air you're breathing.

Teach it to your children. Let it soundtrack their faith as it has for generations before them. Teach them how to pray through each phrase.

Let it disciple your reactions. Anxious? "Give us today . . ."

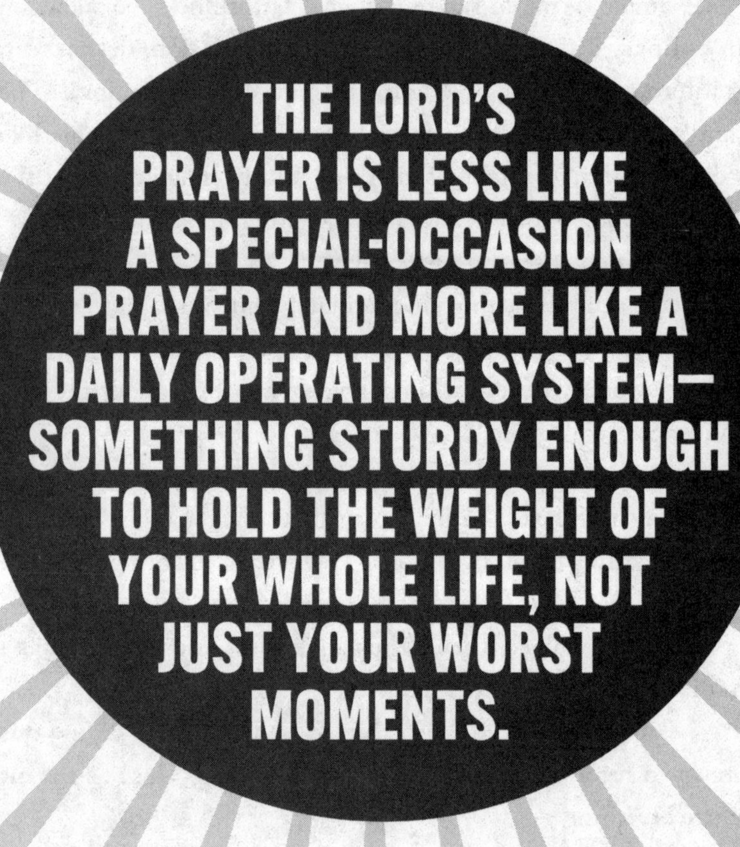
THE LORD'S
PRAYER IS LESS LIKE
A SPECIAL-OCCASION
PRAYER AND MORE LIKE A
DAILY OPERATING SYSTEM—
SOMETHING STURDY ENOUGH
TO HOLD THE WEIGHT OF
YOUR WHOLE LIFE, NOT
JUST YOUR WORST
MOMENTS.

Powerless? "Your kingdom come . . ." Under attack? "Deliver me from evil!"

Let this prayer become the steady rhythm of your life.

This prayer is not a dusty memory verse, not a whispered fall-back, but the framework on which you can build your days. Let it greet your mornings and settle your evenings. Let it be the song that rises when words fail, the compass that points north when you've lost your way.

Why? Because Jesus gave it to us. When the disciples asked, "Teach us to pray," Jesus didn't give them a lecture, a formula, or a seminar. He gave them words. Words to be spoken. Words to be lived. A prayer for ordinary people with ordinary lives.

Here's the mystery: You never outgrow the Lord's Prayer. There is no secret upgrade, no graduate-level version. These words remain—and they are always enough. They are simple enough for a child, deep enough for a theologian, strong enough to hold you for a lifetime.

As you pray these words, day by day, year by year, I pray that they will seep into the cracks of your soul and remake you from the inside out. I pray that you become the kind of person who quietly unnerves the world with your joy, your gentleness, your stubborn hope. I pray that the kingdom of heaven will spill out of you—into your home, your friendships, your city—until the world is a little more like what Jesus had in mind.

May you find, as I have, that this really is the only prayer you need.

TWELVE

A THIRTY-DAY GUIDE TO PRAYING LIKE JESUS

You did it! You read an entire book on prayer! You wrestled with the meaning of each line of the Lord's Prayer. Now it's time to put what you've learned into practice. Here's the invitation: For the next thirty days, pray the entire Lord's Prayer out loud—slowly, intentionally, and from the heart. Every single day.

Here's what that looks like: Each day, you will go through the entirety of the Lord's Prayer one movement at a time. After each movement, simply pray what you've got! Sometimes you might spend most of your time in one section, as I often do, but it's important to hit each movement in order.

In each day of this prayer guide, you'll focus on just one line. Let it get under your skin. Let it form your imagination. Let it shape your actions.

Each day includes:

- A note from me
- The full text of the Lord's Prayer (with one line emphasized for that day's focus)
- A short reflection
- A simple prayer prompt
- A small, tangible spiritual practice

Before we jump into this guide, I have two final pieces of advice:

1. Don't be afraid to start small.

If you can manage only thirty seconds of prayer, that's okay. The important thing is that you come back again tomorrow. If you can't pray all night, then don't. Just start by praying as you can.

2. Pray simply and honestly.

Here's a quote from Jesus himself: "Find a quiet, secluded place. . . . Just be there as simply and honestly as you can manage" (Matthew 6:6 MSG).

As you pray over the next thirty days, remember to use simple words. Practice being honest with God. Bring your real struggles: your doubts, your weaknesses, your fears, your frustrations. Don't try to present a perfect version of yourself.

It's time to jump into day 1. And remember, pray what you've got!

DAY 1

When I first started praying this line, I realized how much of my life I'd spent talking *at* God, not *to* a good Father. It was kind of like conversing with a stranger and awkwardly asking for stuff. But over time, these words—"Our Father"—have become an anchor for something much richer. They remind me that before I achieve anything, fix anything, or pray anything, I'm a son. And sons don't have to perform to be loved.

Take a moment now in a quiet place to pray through the Lord's Prayer slowly:

> ***Our Father in heaven,***
> hallowed be your name,
> your kingdom come,
> your will be done,
>   on earth as it is in heaven.
> Give us today our daily bread.
> And forgive us our debts,
>   as we also have forgiven our debtors.
> And lead us not into temptation,
>   but deliver us from the evil one.

Focus your prayers on this phrase: "Our Father in heaven."

REFLECTION: You are not alone. You are not abandoned. You are God's child. This is where all prayer starts—not with your words but with your relationship to a very good Father.

PRAYER PROMPT: Father, help me see you as kind, near, and good.

SPIRITUAL PRACTICE: Picture God looking at you with deep affection as a father loving his child. Sit quietly in that for a time.

DAY 2

Growing up, I always assumed "in heaven" meant that God was distant. But Jesus meant something far more comforting. He used it to show that God is above us, beyond us, and yet somehow present with us. In other words, he's not limited like we are. Praying this line slowly and several times daily has helped me trade my picture of a far-off God for the reality of a Father who fills every moment with his presence.

Take a moment now in a quiet place to pray through the Lord's Prayer slowly:

> ***Our Father in heaven,***
> hallowed be your name,
> your kingdom come,
> your will be done,
>   on earth as it is in heaven.
> Give us today our daily bread.
> And forgive us our debts,
>   as we also have forgiven our debtors.
> And lead us not into temptation,
>   but deliver us from the evil one.

Focus your prayers on this phrase: "Our Father in heaven."

REFLECTION: God is closer than the air you breathe. He's not distant or disinterested. He's attentive, personal, present.

PRAYER PROMPT: Father, remind me today that you are present in every moment.

SPIRITUAL PRACTICE: Every time you check your phone today, whisper, "You are with me."

DAY 3

For most of my life, "hallowed be your name" felt like a formal line you're supposed to say, something polite before getting to the real prayer. But Jesus meant something far more personal. He was inviting me to see God not as an obligation but as the most beautiful reality in my life. Praying this line slowly and several times a day has helped me shift my focus from my problems to God's presence. This has been a perspective changer. I still have problems, of course—and I bring them to God—but I now find that my problems don't have the final say. When I start with God's beauty instead of my anxiety, something in me settles. My problems are still real, but they're no longer in charge.

Take a moment now in a quiet place to pray through the Lord's Prayer slowly:

> Our Father in heaven,
> ***hallowed be your name,***
> your kingdom come,
> your will be done,
> on earth as it is in heaven.
> Give us today our daily bread.
> And forgive us our debts,
> as we also have forgiven our debtors.
> And lead us not into temptation,
> but deliver us from the evil one.

Focus your prayers on this phrase: "hallowed be your name."

REFLECTION: When you begin with reverence, everything else finds its place. Adoration doesn't ignore your pain—it reframes it.

PRAYER PROMPT: God, show me again what makes you so beautiful.

SPIRITUAL PRACTICE: Go outside. Speak aloud three things that stir awe in you. End by saying, "Holy is your name."

DAY 4

"Hallowed be your name" has quietly become one of the most important parts of this prayer for me. When I pray it slowly throughout the day, I'm reminded that God's name—not my plans, my productivity, or my reputation—is what deserves the highest place in my life. I still have ambitions and responsibilities, but they don't sit in the driver's seat like they used to. Beginning with God's holiness has helped reorder my loves. It brings me back to what matters most.

Take a moment now in a quiet place to pray through the Lord's Prayer slowly:

> Our Father in heaven,
> ***hallowed be your name,***
> your kingdom come,
> your will be done,
>   on earth as it is in heaven.
> Give us today our daily bread.
> And forgive us our debts,
>   as we also have forgiven our debtors.
> And lead us not into temptation,
>   but deliver us from the evil one.

Focus your prayers on this phrase: "hallowed be your name."

REFLECTION: When you see God clearly, you see everything else more clearly too. Holiness isn't about rules, it's about awe.

PRAYER PROMPT: Father, let me see your holiness not as distance but as beauty.

SPIRITUAL PRACTICE: Light a candle today. Let it burn while you pray, offering up your awe at God's goodness and majesty.

DAY 5

For most of my life, I assumed "your kingdom come" just meant "God, make things better." But praying it slowly throughout the day has exposed something deeper in me—I have my own little kingdom I'm always trying to build: my preferences, my plans, my way. This line has become a quiet surrender. I still work hard and make plans, but they don't have the same level of control over me. Asking for God's kingdom first has helped loosen my grip. It brings me back to a better story than the one I'm trying to write on my own.

Take a moment now in a quiet place to pray through the Lord's Prayer slowly:

> Our Father in heaven,
> hallowed be your name,
> ***your kingdom come,***
> your will be done,
>   on earth as it is in heaven.
> Give us today our daily bread.
> And forgive us our debts,
>   as we also have forgiven our debtors.
> And lead us not into temptation,
>   but deliver us from the evil one.

Focus your prayers on this phrase: "your kingdom come."

REFLECTION: God's kingdom means God's way. And often that begins where your preferences end.

PRAYER PROMPT: Jesus, show me where my kingdom is getting in the way of yours.

SPIRITUAL PRACTICE: Take a few minutes to write out a description of your "ideal life." Ask Jesus what he wants to edit.

DAY 6

"Your kingdom come" has become one of the more disruptive parts of this prayer for me—in a good way. Praying it regularly has revealed how often I crowd my days with my own priorities. But something shifts when I pause and invite God's kingdom instead of my own. I still move through busy days and full schedules, but they feel less claustrophobic when I remember I'm part of something bigger. This line helps me make space for God's interruptions, which are usually better than my plans anyway.

Take a moment now in a quiet place to pray through the Lord's Prayer slowly:

> Our Father in heaven,
> hallowed be your name,
> ***your kingdom come,***
> your will be done,
>   on earth as it is in heaven.
> Give us today our daily bread.
> And forgive us our debts,
>   as we also have forgiven our debtors.
> And lead us not into temptation,
>   but deliver us from the evil one.

Focus your prayers on this phrase: "your kingdom come."

REFLECTION: You're not just praying for change; you're part of how it happens.

PRAYER PROMPT: Father, let your kingdom come—in me, in my home, on my street.

SPIRITUAL PRACTICE: Intercede for someone by name. Ask for God's kingdom to touch their life.

DAY 7

Some days, praying, "Your will be done," feels like setting down a heavy backpack I didn't realize I was carrying. I spend so much energy trying to arrange my circumstances, predict outcomes, and manage the future. But when I pray this line quietly, in small moments, it's like I feel the weight shift. My situation doesn't magically change, but my posture does. This prayer gives me permission to stop thinking I have to hold everything together.

Take a moment now in a quiet place to pray through the Lord's Prayer slowly:

> Our Father in heaven,
> hallowed be your name,
> your kingdom come,
> ***your will be done,***
> on earth as it is in heaven.
> Give us today our daily bread.
> And forgive us our debts,
> as we also have forgiven our debtors.
> And lead us not into temptation,
> but deliver us from the evil one.

Focus your prayers on this phrase: "your will be done."

REFLECTION: The goal of prayer is not control, it's consent.

PRAYER PROMPT: Jesus, what are you showing me through this prayer?

SPIRITUAL PRACTICE: Reread the full prayer slowly. Circle one word that stands out.

DAY 8

I've noticed that "your will be done" hits differently now that I'm a dad. I sometimes watch my kids resist what I know is good for them, not because it's bad but because they can't see what I see. Praying this line has become a mirror. It gently reminds me that I do the same thing with God. I still want what I want, but this prayer helps me trust that God sees farther down the road than I can. It makes obedience feel less like loss and more like wisdom.

Take a moment now in a quiet place to pray through the Lord's Prayer slowly:

Our Father in heaven,
hallowed be your name,
your kingdom come,
your will be done,
    on earth as it is in heaven.
Give us today our daily bread.
And forgive us our debts,
    as we also have forgiven our debtors.
And lead us not into temptation,
    but deliver us from the evil one.

Focus your prayers on this phrase: "your will be done."

REFLECTION: God's will is better than yours, even when it hurts.

PRAYER PROMPT: God, not my will today but yours.

SPIRITUAL PRACTICE: Hold your hands open while you pray. Release control.

DAY 9

"Your will be done" has become one of the most clarifying parts of this prayer for me, especially in processing my marriage. Often Mary and I look at the same situation from different angles. Praying this line slowly throughout the day has helped me release the need to always be "right" and instead ask God what he's doing in both of us. I still have strong preferences (just ask Mary), but I'm learning that God's will usually looks like being humble, listening, and choosing unity over winning. This line gently reminds me of that every time.

Take a moment now in a quiet place to pray through the Lord's Prayer slowly:

> Our Father in heaven,
> hallowed be your name,
> your kingdom come,
> ***your will be done,***
> on earth as it is in heaven.
> Give us today our daily bread.
> And forgive us our debts,
> as we also have forgiven our debtors.
> And lead us not into temptation,
> but deliver us from the evil one.

Focus your prayers on this phrase: "your will be done."

REFLECTION: True peace comes from trusting God's wisdom.

PRAYER PROMPT: God, help me want what you want, even when I don't understand.

SPIRITUAL PRACTICE: Name one ungodly thing or relationship you're grasping on to. Surrender it in prayer. Ask the Holy Spirit for clarity about your right next step.

DAY 10

"On earth as it is in heaven" has become one of the most challenging lines for me in this whole prayer. Praying it slowly throughout the day makes me realize how often my reactions look nothing like heaven, especially in the small, unguarded moments at home or at work. But this line also keeps pulling me back to a bigger vision. I still fail to see it plenty of times, but I'm learning to pause and ask, "What would heaven look like here?" It changes how I speak, how I listen, and how I show up. It reminds me that heaven isn't just waiting for me one day; it wants to meet me in the ordinary moments right now.

Take a moment now in a quiet place to pray through the Lord's Prayer slowly:

Our Father in heaven,
hallowed be your name,
your kingdom come,
your will be done,
    on earth as it is in heaven.
Give us today our daily bread.
And forgive us our debts,
    as we also have forgiven our debtors.
And lead us not into temptation,
    but deliver us from the evil one.

Focus your prayers on this phrase: "on earth as it is in heaven."

REFLECTION: Heaven isn't only for later. It begins here.

PRAYER PROMPT: God, help me make my corner of earth a little more like heaven today.

SPIRITUAL PRACTICE: Do one small act of kindness today—quietly, anonymously.

DAY 11

"On earth as it is in heaven" has shaped not just what I do but who I'm becoming on the inside. When I pray it slowly throughout the day, I realize how much of my inner world—my thoughts, my tone, my hurry—still needs heaven's touch. I still drift into impatience and frustration, especially when I'm tired, but this line keeps redirecting me. It invites me to transform my inner life before I try to bring my frustrations anywhere else. And honestly, that shift alone changes the atmosphere around me more than I expect.

Take a moment now in a quiet place to pray through the Lord's Prayer slowly:

> Our Father in heaven,
> hallowed be your name,
> your kingdom come,
> your will be done,
>   ***on earth as it is in heaven.***
> Give us today our daily bread.
> And forgive us our debts,
>   as we also have forgiven our debtors.
> And lead us not into temptation,
>   but deliver us from the evil one.

Focus your prayers on this phrase: "on earth as it is in heaven."

REFLECTION: Heaven begins in hearts surrendered to Jesus.

PRAYER PROMPT: Jesus, begin with me. Reign in my inner life.

SPIRITUAL PRACTICE: Write a short list of heaven's values: peace, joy, healing. Ask God to form one of them in you today.

DAY 12

For a long time, "Give us today our daily bread" felt like a line I didn't quite need. I tend to assume that if something has to get done, I have to make it happen. But praying this line silently or quietly throughout the day has revealed how much pressure I carry that God never asked me to. I still work hard, but I'm learning to release the deeper fear beneath the work—the fear that it's all on me. This line helps me remember that provision starts with God, not with my hustle.

Take a moment now in a quiet place to pray through the Lord's Prayer slowly:

> Our Father in heaven,
> hallowed be your name,
> your kingdom come,
> your will be done,
> on earth as it is in heaven.
> ***Give us today our daily bread.***
> And forgive us our debts,
> as we also have forgiven our debtors.
> And lead us not into temptation,
> but deliver us from the evil one.

Focus your prayers on this phrase: "Give us today our daily bread."

REFLECTION: Jesus invites you to ask for what you need.

PRAYER PROMPT: Father, here's what I need today . . .

SPIRITUAL PRACTICE: List today's needs: spiritual, emotional, financial, vocational, relational. Offer them one by one to God.

DAY 13

What now stands out to me most in "Give us today our daily bread" is the word *us*. Jesus didn't teach me to pray, "Give me today my daily bread." He taught me to pray for *our* daily bread. Praying this slowly throughout the day has opened my eyes to the needs around me. I still take my own needs to God too, but this line keeps expanding my imagination beyond myself. It nudges me to ask, "Who else needs bread today? Who else needs care, encouragement, or provision?" It reminds me that following Jesus is never a solo project. We receive from God together, and we look out for one another along the way.

Take a moment now in a quiet place to pray through the Lord's Prayer slowly:

> Our Father in heaven,
> hallowed be your name,
> your kingdom come,
> your will be done,
> on earth as it is in heaven.
> ***Give us today our daily bread.***
> And forgive us our debts,
> as we also have forgiven our debtors.
> And lead us not into temptation,
> but deliver us from the evil one.

Focus your prayers on this phrase: "Give us today our daily bread."

REFLECTION: God wants to meet not just your needs but your anxieties too.

PRAYER PROMPT: Father, deliver me from the fear that I won't have enough.

SPIRITUAL PRACTICE: Share a small resource with someone today. Start seeing what happens when you live openhanded.

DAY 14

Forgiveness has never come naturally to me. I can hold on to little things longer than I mean to—even stuff I thought I'd already released. But praying, "Forgive us our debts," slowly throughout the day has become a kind of heart check. It reminds me that I stand in constant need of grace too. I still replay conversations in my head or feel that old instinct to defend myself, but this line keeps softening me. It pulls me back to humility. Before I ask God to deal with anyone else's wrongs, I remember the mountain of grace he keeps extending to me. And that changes how I move through the world.

Take a moment now in a quiet place to pray through the Lord's Prayer slowly:

> Our Father in heaven,
> hallowed be your name,
> your kingdom come,
> your will be done,
>   on earth as it is in heaven.
> Give us today our daily bread.
> ***And forgive us our debts,***
>   as we also have forgiven our debtors.
> And lead us not into temptation,
>   but deliver us from the evil one.

Focus your prayers on this phrase: "And forgive us our debts."

REFLECTION: Forgiveness is the gateway to freedom.

PRAYER PROMPT: God, show me what I need to be forgiven for—and help me receive your forgiveness.

SPIRITUAL PRACTICE: Say aloud, "I am forgiven." Write it down. Read it again before bed.

DAY 15

"Forgive us our debts" hits a tender place in me. I can be pretty harsh with myself, being quicker to notice my shortcomings than God's grace. But saying this line slowly many times a day pulls me out of that inner criticism. I still wrestle with my own mistakes, but this prayer reminds me that God doesn't hold them over me. He covers them. He frees me. It keeps teaching my heart that forgiveness isn't something I achieve by trying harder; it's something I receive with open hands.

Take a moment now in a quiet place to pray through the Lord's Prayer slowly:

> Our Father in heaven,
> hallowed be your name,
> your kingdom come,
> your will be done,
>   on earth as it is in heaven.
> Give us today our daily bread.
> ***And forgive us our debts,***
>   as we also have forgiven our debtors.
> And lead us not into temptation,
>   but deliver us from the evil one.

Focus your prayers on this phrase: "And forgive us our debts."

REFLECTION: Forgiveness isn't easy. But it's essential. We don't earn God's forgiveness—it's grace. Pure, undeserved grace.

PRAYER PROMPT: Father, I receive your forgiveness today, not because I deserve it but because you're good.

SPIRITUAL PRACTICE: Psalm 103:12 tells us, "As far as the east is from the west, so far has he removed our transgressions from us." Sit quietly and picture your sins being carried far away. Then say aloud, "I am forgiven."

DAY 16

"As we also have forgiven our debtors" keeps pulling me out of my individualistic way of thinking. Forgiveness isn't just my work, it's *our* work. When I pray this line slowly throughout the day, I'm reminded that I'm part of a community of forgiven people who are learning to forgive together. I still feel resistance in me—plenty of it—but this line keeps nudging me toward grace. It helps me remember that I don't grow spiritually on an island. We forgive together, heal together, and follow Jesus together.

Take a moment now in a quiet place to pray through the Lord's Prayer slowly:

> Our Father in heaven,
> hallowed be your name,
> your kingdom come,
> your will be done,
>   on earth as it is in heaven.
> Give us today our daily bread.
> And forgive us our debts,
>   ***as we also have forgiven our debtors.***
> And lead us not into temptation,
>   but deliver us from the evil one.

Focus your prayers on this phrase: "as we also have forgiven our debtors."

REFLECTION: If we are forgiven people, we must become forgiving people. There's no spiritual growth without this hard work.

PRAYER PROMPT: Lord, help me forgive the one I don't want to forgive.

SPIRITUAL PRACTICE: Write down the name of someone you're holding a grudge against. Pray a blessing over them.

DAY 17

For most of my life, I carried around a large satchel of unforgiveness stuffed with old hurts, little grievances, and the names of people I avoided dealing with. I'd wait until the weight became unbearable and then grudgingly forgive one person. But praying "as we also have forgiven our debtors" several times a day has changed that rhythm. I'm learning to forgive quickly, in real time, instead of stockpiling pain. It's surprisingly freeing. My relational life has simplified: less clutter, less tension, less story-spinning. This line reminds me that forgiveness isn't an event; it's a way of traveling lighter through the day.

Take a moment now in a quiet place to pray through the Lord's Prayer slowly:

> Our Father in heaven,
> hallowed be your name,
> your kingdom come,
> your will be done,
>   on earth as it is in heaven.
> Give us today our daily bread.
> And forgive us our debts,
>   ***as we also have forgiven our debtors.***
> And lead us not into temptation,
>   but deliver us from the evil one.

Focus your prayers on this phrase: "as we also have forgiven our debtors."

REFLECTION: Forgiveness doesn't mean forgetting. It means choosing love over revenge.

PRAYER PROMPT: Lord, I release my desire to get even. Help me walk in your mercy.

SPIRITUAL PRACTICE: Pray the phrase "I choose mercy over memory" throughout the day.

DAY 18

When I was touring with different bands, there were moments backstage when the combination of exhaustion, loneliness, and adrenaline created all kinds of inner temptations—nothing dramatic, just the subtle stuff: escape, numbing, shortcuts. "Lead us not into temptation" has become the prayer I wish I'd prayed then—slowly, several times a day. These days, it helps me notice the moment *before* the compromise, not after. I am still tempted, but this line helps me name what's pulling at me and ask God for a better path forward. It's become a way of staying awake to my own heart.

Take a moment now in a quiet place to pray through the Lord's Prayer slowly:

> Our Father in heaven,
> hallowed be your name,
> your kingdom come,
> your will be done,
>   on earth as it is in heaven.
> Give us today our daily bread.
> And forgive us our debts,
>   as we also have forgiven our debtors.
> ***And lead us not into temptation,***
>   but deliver us from the evil one.

Focus your prayers on this phrase: "And lead us not into temptation."

REFLECTION: Temptation isn't sin, but it is an invitation to sin. We need help before we fall, not just after.

PRAYER PROMPT: Father, guide me away from what will lead me to regret.

SPIRITUAL PRACTICE: Identify your biggest temptation trigger. Make a plan to avoid it today.

DAY 19

There's always a moment before the moment—the split second when I feel myself leaning toward something I'll regret. For years I prayed about temptation only after I'd already given in. But saying this line many times a day has trained me to notice that earlier moment. I am still tempted, of course, but this prayer helps me interrupt the drift. It gives me language for what's happening inside me and invites God into it sooner. It has become one of the ways I practice honesty—naming what's really going on before it becomes something heavier to carry.

Take a moment now in a quiet place to pray through the Lord's Prayer slowly:

> Our Father in heaven,
> hallowed be your name,
> your kingdom come,
> your will be done,
> on earth as it is in heaven.
> Give us today our daily bread.
> And forgive us our debts,
> as we also have forgiven our debtors.
> ***And lead us not into temptation,***
> but deliver us from the evil one.

Focus your prayers on this phrase: "And lead us not into temptation."

REFLECTION: Jesus teaches us to pray proactively. We don't have to wait until we're falling to ask for strength.

PRAYER PROMPT: Holy Spirit, lead me down better paths today.

SPIRITUAL PRACTICE: Be intentional today about pausing and asking, "Is this leading me toward or away from Jesus?"

DAY 20

I used to assume every struggle was either my fault or someone else's. But the longer I follow Jesus, the more I realize that some battles have a darker source. Evil is real, and it aims to discourage, divide, and derail. Praying, "Deliver us from the evil one," many times a day helps me stop pretending everything is purely psychological or circumstantial. I still have agency, of course, but this line reminds me that I also have an enemy—and a Savior who knows how to protect me. It gives me courage to ask for help in places I didn't used to name.

Take a moment now in a quiet place to pray through the Lord's Prayer slowly:

> Our Father in heaven,
> hallowed be your name,
> your kingdom come,
> your will be done,
> on earth as it is in heaven.
> Give us today our daily bread.
> And forgive us our debts,
> as we also have forgiven our debtors.
> And lead us not into temptation,
> ***but deliver us from the evil one.***

Focus your prayers on this phrase: "but deliver us from the evil one."

REFLECTION: Evil is real. But it doesn't have the final word.

PRAYER PROMPT: Jesus, rescue me from everything that would ruin me.

SPIRITUAL PRACTICE: Place your hand over your heart and say, "I am not alone in this battle." Then read through Ephesians 6:10–18 to remind yourself to put on the full armor of God.

DAY 21

"Deliver us from the evil one" has become one of the most sobering lines in this whole prayer for me. I don't love thinking about evil, but pretending it doesn't exist never protected me from it. There really is an enemy who seeks my downfall and destruction, who studies my patterns, who knows the buttons to push, who would love nothing more than to cloud my judgment and fracture my relationships. Praying this line many times a day recenters me in the truth that I'm not fighting these battles alone. Jesus doesn't just forgive me—he shields me, steadies me, and strengthens me in the exact places I'm weakest. This line reminds me that evil is real, but more so is the One who overcomes it.

Take a moment now in a quiet place to pray through the Lord's Prayer slowly:

> Our Father in heaven,
> hallowed be your name,
> your kingdom come,
> your will be done,
>   on earth as it is in heaven.
> Give us today our daily bread.
> And forgive us our debts,
>   as we also have forgiven our debtors.
> And lead us not into temptation,
>   ***but deliver us from the evil one.***

Focus your prayers on this phrase: "but deliver us from the evil one."

REFLECTION: You are part of a story that is still being written. Jesus has overcome. And in him, you will too.

PRAYER PROMPT: God, help me see past what's against me and trust your Spirit within me.

SPIRITUAL PRACTICE: Memorize 1 John 4:4: "You, dear children, are from God and have overcome them, because the one who is in you is greater than the one who is in the world."

DAY 22

Praying the Lord's Prayer for someone I love slows me down in the best way. Each line becomes a kind of doorway: "Father, be close to them . . . Make your kingdom real in their life . . . Give them what they need today . . ." And as I move through the prayer, something in me changes too. I see them with compassion instead of frustration, hope instead of worry. This prayer has become one of the ways God keeps enlarging my heart.

Ask the Holy Spirit who or what to pray for. Then take a moment in a quiet place to pray through the Lord's Prayer, pausing after each phrase and "praying what you've got" about your prayer subject.

> Our Father in heaven,
> hallowed be your name,
> your kingdom come,
> your will be done,
>   on earth as it is in heaven.
> Give us today our daily bread.
> And forgive us our debts,
>   as we also have forgiven our debtors.
> And lead us not into temptation,
>   but deliver us from the evil one.

REFLECTION: As you prayed this prayer for someone you love, notice what shifted in you. Where did compassion replace irritation, or hope crowd out anxiety? The Lord's Prayer doesn't just shape what we ask for others; it quietly reshapes the one who is praying.

PRAYER PROMPT: Father, thank you for loving this person more than I ever could. As I pray your prayer over their life, soften my heart, widen my vision, and teach me to see them the way you do.

SPIRITUAL PRACTICE: Reach out to the person you prayed for today—by text, note, or conversation—and offer a simple word of encouragement or presence, without fixing anything. Let love, not urgency, set the pace.

DAY 23

I've noticed that the Lord's Prayer gets richer when I'm tired or overwhelmed. Not because it magically fixes my circumstances but because it anchors me in the truth that God isn't watching my life from a distance. He walks with me through the confusion, the waiting, the ache, the unanswered parts. This prayer doesn't promise ease, but it does promise companionship. And praying it phrase by phrase has become one of the ways I remember I'm never navigating any of this alone.

Ask the Holy Spirit who or what to pray for. Then take a moment in a quiet place to pray through the Lord's Prayer, pausing after each phrase and "praying what you've got" about your prayer subject.

> Our Father in heaven,
> hallowed be your name,
> your kingdom come,
> your will be done,
>   on earth as it is in heaven.
> Give us today our daily bread.
> And forgive us our debts,
>   as we also have forgiven our debtors.
> And lead us not into temptation,
>   but deliver us from the evil one.

REFLECTION: The Lord's Prayer doesn't promise an easy life, but it does promise that God will walk with us through all of it.

PRAYER PROMPT: Father, help me trust you when the road is long or the answers are slow.

SPIRITUAL PRACTICE: Reflect on the hardest thing you've been through. Thank God that you're still standing.

DAY 24

I've noticed that praying the Lord's Prayer slowly—really slowly—acts like a spiritual reset button. This prayer is not a checklist, not a box to tick, but a way of recentering my scattered heart. By the time I get to the end, the noise inside me has diminished. My priorities feel clearer. My reactions soften. My hurried assumptions are rearranged. This prayer keeps pulling me back to what actually matters, not what feels urgent in the moment. Praying it has become less of a task and more of a daily recalibration of my entire worldview.

Ask the Holy Spirit who or what to pray for. Then take a moment in a quiet place to pray through the Lord's Prayer, pausing after each phrase and "praying what you've got" about your prayer subject.

> Our Father in heaven,
> hallowed be your name,
> your kingdom come,
> your will be done,
> on earth as it is in heaven.
> Give us today our daily bread.
> And forgive us our debts,
> as we also have forgiven our debtors.
> And lead us not into temptation,
> but deliver us from the evil one.

REFLECTION: This prayer is not just a box on a spiritual checklist. It's a worldview, a daily reorientation to what matters most.

PRAYER PROMPT: Realign my desires today, Lord.

SPIRITUAL PRACTICE: Write out the Lord's Prayer by hand. Pray it again slowly, line by line.

DAY 25

As a former touring musician, I know what repetition can do. You practice a part so many times that eventually it becomes muscle memory. I've noticed the same thing happening with this prayer. Repeating it isn't about getting it "right"—it's about letting it sink into the deeper places of me. The more I pray it, the more naturally its rhythms rise up in moments of stress, fear, or joy.

Ask the Holy Spirit who or what to pray for. Then take a moment in a quiet place to pray through the Lord's Prayer, pausing after each phrase and "praying what you've got" about your prayer subject.

> Our Father in heaven,
> hallowed be your name,
> your kingdom come,
> your will be done,
>   on earth as it is in heaven.
> Give us today our daily bread.
> And forgive us our debts,
>   as we also have forgiven our debtors.
> And lead us not into temptation,
>   but deliver us from the evil one.

REFLECTION: There is power in repetition—not as a performance but as formation. Prayer reshapes you.

PRAYER PROMPT: Father, keep shaping me through these ancient, holy words.

SPIRITUAL PRACTICE: Commit to praying the Lord's Prayer every day this week, even after this guide ends.

DAY 26

Praying the Lord's Prayer throughout the day has taught me that God doesn't want to pull me out of the chaos of everyday life; he wants to meet me in it. Whether I'm dealing with parenting moments, tough conversations, or the swirl of responsibilities, this prayer doesn't remove me from the world. It reorients me. It gives me fresh strength to be present, patient, and hopeful in the exact places that used to drain me.

Ask the Holy Spirit who or what to pray for. Then take a moment in a quiet place to pray through the Lord's Prayer, pausing after each phrase and "praying what you've got" about your prayer subject.

> Our Father in heaven,
> hallowed be your name,
> your kingdom come,
> your will be done,
>   on earth as it is in heaven.
> Give us today our daily bread.
> And forgive us our debts,
>   as we also have forgiven our debtors.
> And lead us not into temptation,
>   but deliver us from the evil one.

REFLECTION: Prayer is not a tool to escape the world; it's a way to engage it with renewed perspective and strength.

PRAYER PROMPT: Lord, send me into my day today as someone who has prayed.

SPIRITUAL PRACTICE: Before checking your phone or email today, pray the Lord's Prayer.

DAY 27

I've learned that praying the Lord's Prayer again and again isn't about convincing God to do something; it's about letting God do something in me. The more I pray these words slowly, honestly, the more they gently reshape my reactions, my desires, and even my default settings. The change isn't dramatic, but it's real. And it's one of the quiet ways God keeps forming me into someone who lives what I pray.

Ask the Holy Spirit who or what to pray for. Then take a moment in a quiet place to pray through the Lord's Prayer, pausing after each phrase and "praying what you've got" about your prayer subject.

> Our Father in heaven,
> hallowed be your name,
> your kingdom come,
> your will be done,
>   on earth as it is in heaven.
> Give us today our daily bread.
> And forgive us our debts,
>   as we also have forgiven our debtors.
> And lead us not into temptation,
>   but deliver us from the evil one.

REFLECTION: When we pray like Jesus, we begin to live like Jesus. Prayer isn't just words; it's an invitation to become someone new.

PRAYER PROMPT: Keep forming me, Jesus. I want to live like you taught me to pray.

SPIRITUAL PRACTICE: Ask someone close to you, "Have you noticed any changes in me lately?" Be open to what they have to say.

DAY 28

I can look back now and see times when God answered my prayers, just not in the way I asked. Some doors closed that I begged him to open; some paths opened that I never would've chosen. And yet, in hindsight, I can see his kindness woven through all of it. This prayer has become my reminder that God isn't passive or indifferent. He hears. He responds. Sometimes he surprises me. Sometimes he saves me from what I thought I wanted.

Ask the Holy Spirit who or what to pray for. Then take a moment in a quiet place to pray through the Lord's Prayer, pausing after each phrase and "praying what you've got" about your prayer subject.

> Our Father in heaven,
> hallowed be your name,
> your kingdom come,
> your will be done,
>   on earth as it is in heaven.
> Give us today our daily bread.
> And forgive us our debts,
>   as we also have forgiven our debtors.
> And lead us not into temptation,
>   but deliver us from the evil one.

REFLECTION: There is no such thing as wasted prayer. God hears. God acts. God answers—sometimes in ways we don't expect.

PRAYER PROMPT: Father, I trust that you've heard every word I've prayed this month.

SPIRITUAL PRACTICE: Take five minutes to sit in silence. Let God speak—no asking, no striving.

DAY 29

Over the last year, the Lord's Prayer has grounded my worries, steadied my desires, and reminded me of the story I belong to. It's no longer just how I begin prayer; it's how I return to who God is and who I'm becoming. These ancient words keep shaping an ordinary life into a God-centered one.

Ask the Holy Spirit who or what to pray for. Then take a moment in a quiet place to pray through the Lord's Prayer, pausing after each phrase and "praying what you've got" about your prayer subject.

> Our Father in heaven,
> hallowed be your name,
> your kingdom come,
> your will be done,
>   on earth as it is in heaven.
> Give us today our daily bread.
> And forgive us our debts,
>   as we also have forgiven our debtors.
> And lead us not into temptation,
>   but deliver us from the evil one.

REFLECTION: The Lord's Prayer is not just the beginning of prayer; it's the foundation for a whole life with God.

PRAYER PROMPT: Thank you for the gift of this prayer, Jesus. Help me carry it for the rest of my life.

SPIRITUAL PRACTICE: Write down your own version of the Lord's Prayer—phrase by phrase, in your own words.

DAY 30

I used to treat the Lord's Prayer like something to graduate from, an early step in faith before moving on to "deeper things." But praying it slowly many times a day has convinced me it's the opposite. This prayer isn't something you outgrow; it's something you grow into. Line by line, it keeps shaping my imagination for who God is, who I am, and how life with him actually works.

Ask the Holy Spirit who or what to pray for. Then take a moment in a quiet place to pray through the Lord's Prayer, pausing after each phrase and "praying what you've got" about your prayer subject.

> Our Father in heaven,
> hallowed be your name,
> your kingdom come,
> your will be done,
> on earth as it is in heaven.
> Give us today our daily bread.
> And forgive us our debts,
> as we also have forgiven our debtors.
> And lead us not into temptation,
> but deliver us from the evil one.

REFLECTION: This is not the end. It's the beginning. Let this prayer become the framework for every season of your life.

PRAYER PROMPT: Keep me close, Lord. Never let me believe I've outgrown this prayer.

SPIRITUAL PRACTICE: Commit to one next step: using the Lord's Prayer for daily prayer, praying it with a prayer partner, or praying it with your family.

ACKNOWLEDGMENTS

My thanks go out to the many people who helped this book become a reality.

To John Raymond, the first person in publishing who heard me preach and told me, “Matt, I think you’re capable of writing a book one day.” Those words stayed with me. Thank you for your friendship, your coaching, and your willingness to slide my first draft across the table to your colleagues at Zondervan Books. I owe you a lifetime of fancy coffee.

To Josh Smallbone and Byron Williamson, whose single conversation took this from “I think this might be an okay idea” to “All right then . . . we’re doing this.”

To the selfless souls who read early drafts—Mum and Dad, Mary, Beth, Josh, Ashley, and Lozza—thank you for your time and your candor.

To Keren Baltzer, the coolest editor in the biz, thank you for your instincts, your creativity, and for keeping things light.

To Daniel Marrs, thank you for believing that this project

had a home at Zondervan Books and quite literally putting your autograph on the dotted line.

To Rachel Shaver, thank you for making sure people hear about this book. The world needs more marketers like you—thoughtful, hopeful, and genuinely excited about helping people find answers to their important questions.

To the Inglewood lads, thank you for the endless coffees at Dose and for being the kind of mates who work hard, dream big, and love your families well.

To Darren and Derek, thank you for your leadership at Church of the City and for creating a culture where honest prayer is welcome.

To my little brother and gifted lawyer, Michael Smallbone, thank you for all the free advice. Our next lunch is on you.

To Mum, Dad, Sue, and Kate, thank you for the group text subtitle brainstorming session. We tried real hard.

To Mary, Isaac, Caleb, Jack, and Eliana—you are my entire world, the best part of my fantastic life. Thank you for letting me tell our family's stories.

And finally, to the world's coolest congregation—Church of the City, Downtown Nashville: This book was written with you legends in mind. Let's go and see the fame and deeds of God repeated in our days!

NOTES

INTRODUCTION: THE PRAYER STRUGGLE (YOU ARE HERE)

1. David Martyn Lloyd-Jones, *Studies in the Sermon on the Mount* (Grand Rapids: Eerdmans, 1959), loc. 5419, Kindle.
2. C. S. Lewis, *The Problem of Pain* (New York: HarperCollins, 2009), 23, Kindle.

CHAPTER 1: HOW *NOT* TO PRAY

1. Michael J. Wilkins, *Matthew*, NIV Application Commentary (Grand Rapids: Zondervan, 2004), 272, Kindle.
2. Wilkins, *Matthew*, 274, Kindle.
3. Dallas Willard, *The Divine Conspiracy: Rediscovering Our Hidden Life in God* (New York: HarperCollins, 2009), 215, Kindle.
4. C. S. Lewis, *Letters to Malcolm, Chiefly on Prayer* (New York: HarperCollins, 2017), 27, Kindle.

CHAPTER 2: THE ATTENTIVE FATHER

1. David Martyn Lloyd-Jones, *Studies in the Sermon on the Mount* (Grand Rapids: Eerdmans, 1959), loc. 5584, Kindle.

2. Joachim Jeremias, *Jesus and the Message of the New Testament* (Minneapolis: Fortress Press, 1977), loc. 855, Kindle.
3. Timothy Keller, *Prayer: Experiencing Awe and Intimacy with God* (New York: Penguin, 2016), 69, Kindle.
4. Blue Letter Bible, "Lexicon: Strong's H7355—*raham*," accessed August 17, 2025, https://www.blueletterbible.org/lexicon/h7355/kjv/wlc/0-1/.
5. Leif Hetland, *Healing the Orphan Spirit* (Shippensburg, PA: Destiny Image, 2003).
6. Max Lucado, "A Story of Post-War Orphans and the Promise of Provision," sermon illustration retold in various messages, c. 1990s.

CHAPTER 3: THE FATHER WHO IS AS CLOSE AS AIR

1. David B. Yaden, Jonathan Iwry, Marianna Slack, et al., "The Overview Effect: Awe and Self-Transcendent Experience in Space Flight," *Frontiers in Psychology* 7 (2016).
2. Blue Letter Bible, "Lexicon: Strong's G3772—*ouranos*," accessed July 17, 2025, https://www.blueletterbible.org/lexicon/g3772/niv/mgnt/0-1/.
3. Blue Letter Bible, "Lexicon: Strong's G3772—*ouranos*."
4. Dallas Willard, *The Divine Conspiracy: Rediscovering Our Hidden Life in God* (New York: HarperCollins, 2009), 78, Kindle.
5. Vintage Church LA, "Prayer: Talking to God | John Mark Comer," YouTube video, 45:47, posted October 16, 2023, https://youtu.be/GIYUPIAngGs?si=45ooPl2fsv3nZtbc.
6. Augustine, *Confessions*, Book III, in various translations. Classic Latin: *interior intimo meo* ("more inward than my inmost self") and *superior summo meo* ("higher than my highest"). See, e.g.,

Augustine, *Confessions*, trans. Henry Chadwick (Oxford: Oxford University Press, 1991), 43.

7. Blue Letter Bible, "Lexicon: Strong's G3306—*menō*," accessed October 11, 2025, https://www.blueletterbible.org/lexicon/g3306/niv/mgnt/0-1/.
8. Corrie ten Boom with Elizabeth Sherrill and John Sherrill, *The Hiding Place: The Inspiring True Story of Faith and Forgiveness During World War II*, 35th Anniversary ed. (Grand Rapids: Chosen Books, 2006), Kindle.
9. Ten Boom, *The Hiding Place*, 8, Kindle.

CHAPTER 4: THE RESPECTED AND ASTONISHING FATHER

1. *Merriam-Webster Dictionary*, "hallow," accessed December 1, 2025, https://www.merriam-webster.com/dictionary/hallow.
2. Timothy Keller, *Prayer: Experiencing Awe and Intimacy with God* (New York: Penguin, 2016), 111, Kindle.
3. Paraphrasing Francis Collins in Francis S. Collins, *The Language of God: A Scientist Presents Evidence for Belief* (New York: Free Press, 2006).
4. Timothy Keller and Kathy Keller, *The Meaning of Marriage: Facing the Complexities of Commitment with the Wisdom of God* (New York: Penguin, 2011), 95, Kindle.
5. John Chapman, *Spiritual Letters*, ed. Roger Hudleston (London: Sheed & Ward, 1929).

CHAPTER 5: A CLASH OF KINGDOMS

1. N. T. Wright, *Matthew for Everyone, Part 1: Chapters 1–15* (Louisville, KY: Society for Promoting Christian Knowledge, 2004), 28, Kindle.

2. Michael J. Wilkins, *Matthew*, NIV Application Commentary (Grand Rapids: Zondervan, 2004), 276, Kindle.
3. Dallas Willard, *The Divine Conspiracy: Rediscovering Our Hidden Life in God* (New York: HarperCollins, 2009), 33, Kindle.
4. Willard, *The Divine Conspiracy*, 33, Kindle.
5. John Ortberg, *God Is Closer Than You Think: How Intimacy with God Can Happen Right Now* (Grand Rapids: Zondervan, 2005), 165, Kindle.
6. N. T. Wright, *The Lord and His Prayer* (Grand Rapids: Eerdmans, 1996), 13, Kindle.
7. Quoted in 24-7 Prayer, "Intercession | The Prayer Course—Session 4," YouTube video, 20:00, posted July 13, 2017, https://www.youtube.com/watch?v=GuU2cZ5uCfA.
8. Willard, *The Divine Conspiracy*, 268, Kindle.
9. Pete Greig, *How to Pray: A Simple Guide for Normal People* (Colorado Springs: NavPress, 2019), 100, Kindle.

CHAPTER 6: WHEN THE FATHER'S PLAN IS BEST

1. D. A. Carson, *The Gospel According to John*, Pillar New Testament Commentary (Grand Rapids: Eerdmans, 1991), 497, Kindle.
2. N. T. Wright, *John for Everyone, Part 2: Chapters 11–21*, 20th anniv. ed. with study guide (London: SPCK, 2023), 45, Kindle.
3. Blaise Pascal, *Pensées*, trans. A. J. Krailsheimer (London: Penguin, 1995), no. 512.
4. Pete Greig, *God on Mute: Engaging the Silence of Unanswered Prayer* (Bloomington, MN: Bethany House, 2007), 134–57, Kindle.
5. P. T. Forsyth, *The Soul of Prayer* (Vancouver, Canada: Regent College, 2002), 12, Kindle.

CHAPTER 7: THE GREAT ADVENTURE OF DAILY BREAD

1. Carl R. Trueman, *The Rise and Triumph of the Modern Self: Cultural Amnesia, Expressive Individualism, and the Road to Sexual Revolution* (Wheaton, IL: Crossway, 2020), 372, Kindle.
2. Mother Teresa, *The Joy in Loving: A Guide to Daily Living* (New York: Penguin Compass, 1996), 337, Kindle.
3. Joachim Jeremias, *Jesus and the Message of the New Testament* (Minneapolis: Fortress Press, 1977), Kindle.
4. Blue Letter Bible, "Lexicon: Strong's G1967—*epiousios*," accessed February 14, 2025, https://www.blueletterbible.org/lexicon/g1967/niv/mgnt/0-1/.
5. Blue Letter Bible, "Lexicon: Strong's H3899—*leḥem*," accessed February 14, 2025, https://www.blueletterbible.org/lexicon/h3899/kjv/wlc/0-1/.
6. Timothy Keller, *Prayer: Experiencing Awe and Intimacy with God* (New York: Penguin, 2016), 233, Kindle.
7. Darrell L. Bock, *Luke*, NIV Application Commentary (Grand Rapids: Zondervan, 1994), 310, Kindle.
8. Bock, *Luke*, 311, Kindle.
9. Myron Augsburger, *Matthew*, vol. 24 of The Preacher's Commentary (Nashville: Thomas Nelson, 1985), 91, Kindle.
10. Bruce W. Longenecker, "A Humorous Jesus? Orality, Structure and Characterisation in Luke 14:15–24, and Beyond," *Biblical Interpretation: A Journal of Contemporary Approaches* 16, no. 2 (2008): 179–204.
11. Bock, *Luke*, 311, Kindle.
12. Craig S. Keener, *The IVP Bible Background Commentary: New Testament* (Downers Grove, IL: InterVarsity Press, 1993), 62, Kindle.
13. John M. Frame, *Salvation Belongs to the Lord: An Introduction to*

Systematic Theology (Phillipsburg, NJ: P&R Publishing, 2006), loc. 3308, Kindle.

CHAPTER 8: A TWO-WAY STREET CALLED FORGIVENESS

1. Timothy Keller, *Forgive: Why Should I and How Can I?* (New York: Viking, 2022), 168–70, Kindle.
2. Darren Whitehead, "How to Forgive," YouTube video, 1:26:50, posted July 26, 2024, https://www.youtube.com/watch?v=_IRzQM5-eFE.
3. Blue Letter Bible, "Lexicon: Strong's G5483—*charizomai*," accessed August 13, 2025, https://www.blueletterbible.org/lexicon/g5483/kjv/tr/0-1/.
4. Michael J. Wilkins, *Matthew*, NIV Application Commentary (Grand Rapids: Zondervan, 2004), 622, Kindle.
5. Ronald Rolheiser, *Sacred Fire: A Vision for a Deeper Human and Christian Maturity* (New York: Image Books, 2014), 161, Kindle.
6. Paul Herman, "The Night of the Storm: The St James Church Massacre Retold, 30 Years Later," News24, July 26, 2023, https://specialprojects.news24.com/the-night-of-the-storm-the-st-james-church-massacre-retold-30-years-later/index.html.
7. Herman, "The Night of the Storm."
8. Herman, "The Night of the Storm."
9. Karen Swartz, "Forgiveness: Your Health Depends on It," *Johns Hopkins Medicine Health Library*, Johns Hopkins Medicine, July 2019, https://www.hopkinsmedicine.org/health/wellness-and-prevention/forgiveness-your-health-depends-on-it.
10. Corrie ten Boom and Jamie Buckingham, *Tramp for the Lord* (Grand Rapids: Chosen Books, 1974), 60, Kindle.
11. David A. Stoop, *Forgiving What You'll Never Forget* (Grand Rapids: Revell, 2011), Kindle.

CHAPTER 9: TEMPTATION

1. Donald A. Hagner, *Matthew 1–13*, vol. 33A of Word Biblical Commentary (Dallas: Word Books, 1993), 151, Kindle.
2. N. T. Wright, *The Lord and His Prayer* (Grand Rapids: Eerdmans, 1996), 52, Kindle.
3. Quoted in Good News, "Gospel in Life—Session 3," YouTube video, 11:53, February 5, 2020, https://www.youtube.com/watch?v=vJ9ZfOnacOM.
4. Quoted in "The Sermon on the Mount: A 21-Day Guide to the Greatest Sermon Ever Preached—Day 17 of 21," YouVersion, accessed January 13, 2026, https://www.bible.com/reading-plans/50211-the-sermon-on-the-mount/day/17.
5. John Mark Comer, *Live No Lies: Recognize and Resist the Three Enemies That Sabotage Your Peace* (Colorado Springs: WaterBrook, 2021), 121, Kindle.

CHAPTER 10: OUR SKIRMISH WITH EVIL

1. Timothy Keller, "Spiritual Warfare," *Gospel in Life* podcast, July 3, 2012, https://podcast.gospelinlife.com/e/spiritual-warfare-1562113890/.
2. The Prayer Course, "Session 8: Spiritual Warfare," PrayerCourse.org, accessed February 10, 2025, https://prayercourse.org/session/spiritual-warfare/.
3. C. S. Lewis, *The Screwtape Letters* (New York: HarperCollins, 2001), 6, Kindle.
4. Klyne Snodgrass, *Ephesians*, NIV Application Commentary (Grand Rapids: Zondervan, 1996), 339, Kindle.

From the Publisher

GREAT BOOKS

ARE EVEN BETTER WHEN THEY'RE SHARED!

Help other readers find this one

- Post a review at your favorite online bookseller
- Post a picture on a social media account and share why you enjoyed it
- Send a note to a friend who would also love it—or better yet, give them a copy

Thanks for reading!